MATHEMATICS STUDY MATERIAL

With

Formulas

Chapter-wise Worksheets for Practice

Sample Question papers

CLASS VII

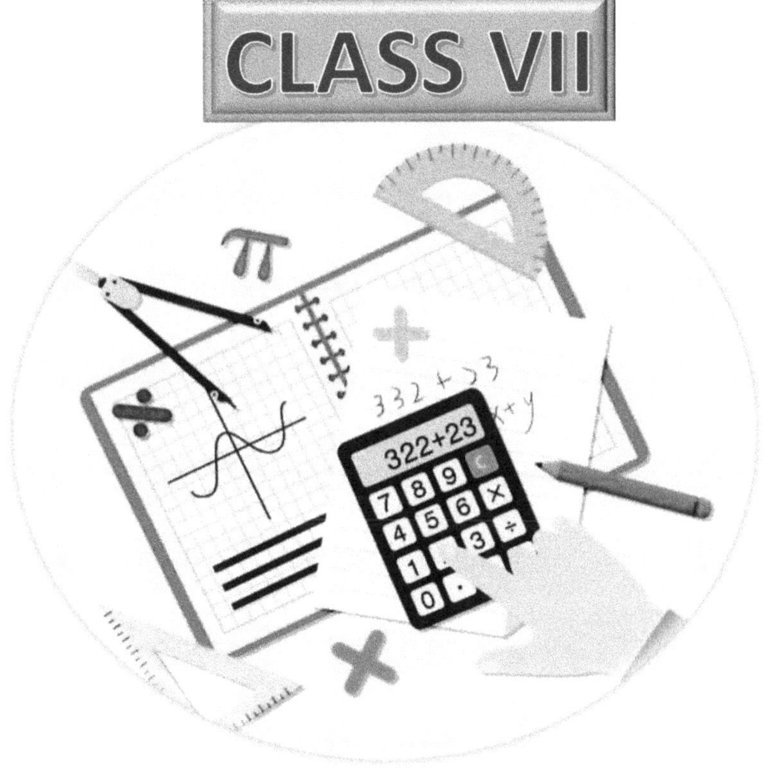

Mala Shekhar

Contents

FORMULAS

The formulas:

Integers Formulas	1. a – b = a + (– b) = a + additive inverse of b 2. a – (– b) = a + b = a + additive inverse of (– b) 3. a + (b + c) = (a + b) + c 4. a × (– b) = (– a) × b = – (a × b) 5. (– a) × (– b) = a × b 6. (a × b) × c = a × (b × c) 7. a × (b + c) = a × b + a × c 8. a × (b – c) = a × b – a × c 9. a ÷ (–b) = (– a) ÷ b where b ≠ 0 10. (– a) ÷ (– b) = a ÷ b where b ≠ 0 11. a ÷ 0 is not defined & a ÷ 1 = a
Fractions and Decimals	1. **Product of two fraction = product of numerators / Product of denominators.** Example: 7/4 × 4/5 = (7 × 4)/(4 × 5) = 28/20 = 7/5 2. **Adding fractions with whole numbers** (a+bc)(a+bc) = (a×c)+bc(a×c)+bc 3. **Adding fractions with like denominators** (ab+db)(ab+db)=(a+d)b(a+d)b 4. **Adding fractions with different denominators** (ab+cd)(ab+cd)=(a×d+b×cb×d)(a×d+b×cb×d) 5. **Adding fractions with variables** abx+cbx=(ab+cb)x=(a+cb)xabx+cbx =(ab+cb)x =(a+cb)x Where: • a, b, c, and, d are constants • x is variable. 6. **To multiply a decimal number by 10, 100 or 1000,** we move the decimal point in the number to the right by as many places as there are zeros over 1. Thus 0.69 × 10 = 6.9, 0.69 × 100 = 69, 0.69 × 1000 = 690 decimal numbers = 0.6 × 0.9 = 0.54 7. **Division of a decimal number** – To divide a decimal number by a whole number, we first divide them as whole numbers. Then place the decimal point in the quotient as in the decimal number. example 12.4 ÷ 4 = 3.1

Simple Equations **&** **Simple Linear Equations**	Equation which has mathematical expression on both sides along with at-least one variable and an equal sign (=) is known as **SIMPLE EQUATIONS**. **Whereas,** A mathematical equation which has mathematical expression on both sides along with two variables and an equal sign (=) is known as **LINEAR EQUATIONS**. For example: $k + 7 = 10$ $K = 10 - 7$ $\Rightarrow k = 3$ An equation is a condition on a variable such that two expressions in the variable should have equal value. Example: $5x + 6 = 26$, the LHS and RHS must be balanced therefore to balance the equation the value of x should be 4. The above equation can be solved as $\Rightarrow 5x = 26 - 6$ $\Rightarrow 5x = 20$ $\Rightarrow x = 205$ $\Rightarrow x = 4$ **Simple Linear Equations** $ax + by + c = 0$, where a, b, and c are any real numbers and x and y are the variables. Example: $3x - 4y = 8$. & $5y + 2 = 3x$.
Lines and Angles	**Two adjacent angles:** Have a common vertex and a common arm but no common interior. **Linear pair:** Adjacent and supplementary. **Two complementary angles:** Measures add up to 90° (sum of 90°) **Two supplementary angles:** Measures add up to 180° (sum of 180°) **Acute angle**: An angle is considered acute if it is less than 90°. Here, $(\angle ABC = 40^\circ) < 90^\circ$ **Obtuse angle**: An angle is obtuse if it is greater than 90° but less than 180°. Here, $90^\circ < (\angle ABC = 117^\circ) < 180^\circ$ **Right angle**: An angle is right angle when its measurement is equals 90°. Here, $\angle ABC = 90^\circ$ **Straight angle**: An angle shows a straight-line angle if its measurement is 180°. Here, $\angle AOB = 180^\circ$ **Reflex angle**: An angle is categorized as a reflex angle if it is greater than 180° but less than 360°. $180^\circ < (\text{Reflex Angle} = 330^\circ) < 360^\circ$

<table>
<tr><td></td><td>
Complete angle: An angle is referred to as a complete angle when its measurement amounts to 360o.
Angle = 360o
• 0°< Acute angle < 90°
• 90°< Obtuse angle < 180°
• 180° < Reflex angle < 360°
• A right angle is equal to 90°
• A straight angle is equal to 180°.
Vertically Opposite angles: When two straight lines intersect each other, they form four angles. Out of four angles the two angles which are directly opposite to each other are called vertically opposite angles. These two vertically opposite angles are always equal.

Exterior angles: Exterior angles are formed at points on the exterior sides (outside angles of 2 parallel lines) of the two lines where a transversal line intersects these two lines.

Interior angles: Interior angles are formed at points on the interior sides (inside angles of 2 parallel lines) of the two lines where a transversal line intersects these two lines.

Alternate angles: Alternate angles are formed when a transversal line cuts through two parallel or non-parallel lines. These angles are a pair of angles which can exist on the interior or exterior sides of the two lines.

Corresponding angles: A pair of angles is called corresponding angles in which one arm of both angles is on the same side of transversal and their other arms are directed in the same sense.
If lines l and m are parallel, then pairs of corresponding angles are equal.

Linear pair of angles

When sum of two adjacent angles is 180°, they are called linear pair of angles.
Or, we can say when supplementary angles formed on a straight line, those angles are called a linear pair of angles.
</td></tr>
<tr><td>The Triangle and its Properties</td><td>
For a triangle ABC:
Sides: AB, BC, CA
Angles: ∠BAC, ∠ABC, ∠BCA
Vertices: A, B, C
For a right-angled triangle QPR, right angles at P:
Pythagoras property $(QR)^2 = (PQ)^2 + (PR)^2$
"In a right-angled triangle, the square on the hypotenuse = sum of the squares on the legs "

• The sum of all interior angles of any triangle is equal to <u>180°</u>
</td></tr>
</table>

<table>
<tr><td></td><td>

- The sum of all exterior angles of any triangle is equal to <u>360°</u>

Six types of triangles: -

1. Acute Angled Triangle → A triangle that has all three angles less than 90° is an acute angle triangle.
2. Right-Angled Triangle → A triangle that has one angle that measures exactly 90° is a right-angle triangle.
3. obtuse Angled Triangle → A triangle that has one angle that measures more than 90° is an obtuse angle triangle
4. Scalene Angled Triangle → A triangle that has all three sides of different lengths is a scalene triangle.
5. Isosceles Angled Triangle → A triangle that has two sides of the same length and the third side of a different length is an isosceles triangle.
6. Equilateral Angled triangle → A triangle that has all three sides of the same length is an equilateral triangle.
7. Altitude → An altitude is a perpendicular bisector on any side of a triangle and it measures the distance between the vertex and the line which is the opposite side.
8. Median → A Mmedian is a line segment that connects a vertex to the central point of the opposite side. Hence, a median needs not to be perpendicular every time.

</td></tr>
<tr><td>Congruence of Triangles</td><td>

Congruent triangles are triangles that are perfect copies of one another.

The different criteria used to prove congruency between two triangles are:

- SSS Criteria: Side-Side-Side
- SAS Criteria: Side-Angle-Side
- ASA Criteria: Angle-Side-Angle
- AAS Criteria: Angle-Angle-Side
- RHS Criteria: Right angle- Hypotenuse-Side

</td></tr>
<tr><td>Comparing Quantities</td><td>

Simple Interest SI = P × R × T / 100
Where P=Principal, T= Time in years, R=Rate of interest per annum
Rate R = SI × 100 / P × T
Principal P = SI × 100 / R×T
Time T= SI × 100 / P × R
Discount = MP-SP

</td></tr>
</table>

	Principal = Amount – Simple Interest • **Profit** = Selling price – Cost price • **Loss** = Cost price – Selling price • If Selling Price (SP) > Cost Price (CP), then it's a profit. • If SP = CP, then it's neither profit nor loss. • If CP > SP, then it's a loss. • SP $= \frac{(100 + \text{Gain }\%)}{100}\ X\ CP$, (when gain% is given) • SP $= \frac{(100 - \text{Loss }\%)}{100}\ X\ CP,$ (when loss% is given) • CP $= \frac{(\text{S.P X } 100)}{100+Gain\ \%}$, (when gain% is given) • CP $= \frac{(\text{S.P X } 100)}{100-Loss\ \%}$, (when loss% is given) • **Discount** = Marked Price – Sale Price • **Discount %** = (Discount / Marked Price) × 100 • **Gain /Profit %** = (Profit / Cost Price) × 100 • **Loss %** = (Loss / Cost Price) × 100 • **Percentage Increased** = Change in Value / Original Value • **Simple Interest** = (Principal × Rate × Time) / 100 • **Compound Interest** = Amount – Principal • When compound interest is compounded annually, • $A = P(1+R/100)^n$ CI = A – P • Sales Tax or VAT = Tax on Selling Price = (Cost Price × Rate of Sales Tax) / 100 • Billing Amount = Selling price + VAT
RATIONAL NUMBERS	• **Commutative Property – Addition**: For any rational numbers a and b, a + b = b + a. • **Commutative Property – Subtraction**: For any rational numbers a and b, a – b ≠ b – a. • **Commutative Property – Multiplication**: For any rational numbers a and b, (a x b) = (b x a). • **Commutative Property – Division**: For any rational numbers a and b, (a/b) ≠ (b/a). • **Associative Property – Addition**: For any rational numbers a, b, and c, *(a + b)* + c = *a* + *(b + c)*.

	• **Associative Property – Subtraction**: For any rational numbers a, b, and c, $(a - b) - c \neq a - (b - c)$ • **Associative Property – Multiplication**: For any rational number a, b, and c, $(a \times b) \times c = a \times (b \times c)$. • **Associative Property – Division**: For any rational numbers a, b, and c, $(a / b) / c \neq a / (b / c)$. • **Distributive Property:** For any three rational numbers *a*, *b* and *c*, $a \times (b + c) = (a \times b) + (a \times c)$.
Ratio and Proportion	**Ratio:** The ratio of two quantities *a* and *b* in the same units, is the fraction $\frac{a}{b}$ and we write it as $a : b$. **Proportion:** The equality of two ratios is called proportion. The proportion can be classified into the following categories, such as: • Direct Proportion • Inverse Proportion • Continued Proportion If $a : b = c : d$, we write $a : b :: c : d$ and we say that *a, b, c, d* are in proportion. **Fourth Proportional:** If $a : b = c : d$, then *d* is called the fourth proportional to *a, b, c*. **Third Proportional:** $a : b = c : d$, then *c* is called the third proportion to *a* and *b*. **If a:b is a ratio, then:** • $a^2:b^2$ is a duplicate ratio • $\sqrt{a}:\sqrt{b}$ is the sub-duplicate ratio • $a^3:b^3$ is a triplicate ratio
Algebraic Expressions	• $a^2 - b^2 = (a - b)(a + b)$ • $(a + b)^2 = a^2 + 2ab + b^2$ • $a^2 + b^2 = (a + b)^2 - 2ab$ • $(a - b)^2 = a^2 - 2ab + b^2$ • $(a + b + c)^2 = a^2 + b^2 + c^2 + 2ab + 2bc + 2ca$ • $(a - b - c)^2 = a^2 + b^2 + c^2 - 2ab + 2bc - 2ca$ • $(a + b)^3 = a^3 + 3a^2b + 3ab^2 + b^3$; $(a + b)^3 = a^3 + b^3 + 3ab(a + b)$ • $(a - b)^3 = a^3 - 3a^2b + 3ab^2 - b^3 = a^3 - b^3 - 3ab(a - b)$ • $a^3 - b^3 = (a - b)(a^2 + ab + b^2)$

	• $a^3 + b^3 = (a + b)(a^2 - ab + b^2)$ • $(a + b)^4 = a^4 + 4a^3b + 6a^2b^2 + 4ab^3 + b^4$ • $(a - b)^4 = a^4 - 4a^3b + 6a^2b^2 - 4ab^3 + b^4$ • $a^4 - b^4 = (a - b)(a + b)(a^2 + b^2)$ • $a^5 - b^5 = (a - b)(a^4 + a^3b + a^2b^2 + ab^3 + b^4)$ • If n is a natural number $a^n - b^n = (a - b)(a^{n-1} + a^{n-2}b+...+ b^{n-2}a + b^{n-1})$ • If n is even (n = 2k), $a^n + b^n = (a + b)(a^{n-1} - a^{n-2}b +...+ b^{n-2}a - b^{n-1})$ • If n is odd (n = 2k + 1), $a^n + b^n = (a + b)(a^{n-1} - a^{n-2}b +a^{n-3}b^2...- b^{n-2}a + b^{n-1})$ • $(a + b + c + ...)^2 = a^2 + b^2 + c^2 + ... + 2(ab + ac + bc + ...)$ • Laws of Exponents $(a^m)(a^n) = a^{m+n}$; $(ab)^m = a^mb^m$; $(a^m)^n = a^{mn}$ • Fractional Exponents $a^0 = 1$
Percentage and its Applications	To change Percentage as fraction: 25% = 25/100 = 1/4 To find Percentage of fraction: 4/7 = 4/7 * 100 To find Percentage of decimal : 0.004 = 4/1000 * 100 To find Percentage of fraction: 4/7 = 4/7*100 To find Percentage of ratio : 4 : 7 = 4/7 *100 Percentages to fractions and ratios = fractions we have to divide by 100 i.e. 25% = 25/100 = 1/4 ratio = 1:4 when some % of total : i.e. 25% of 10 kg Here, 25% of 10 Kg can be expressed as (25 × 10) / 100 = 250/100 = 2.5 Kg
Practical Geometry	**Formulas for 2D Geometry:** • Perimeter of a Square = 4 × Side • Perimeter of a Rectangle = 2 × (Length + Breadth) • Area of a Square = $Side^2$ • Area of a Rectangle = Length × Breadth • Area of a Triangle = ½ × Base × Height • Area of a Trapezoid = ½ × ($Base_1$ + $Base_2$) × Height • Area of a Circle = $A = \pi \times r^2$ • Circumference of a Circle = $2\pi r$

<table>
<tr><td></td><td>Formulas for 3D Geometry:
• Curved Surface Area of a Cylinder = $2\pi rh$
• Total Surface Area of a Cylinder = $2\pi r(r + h)$
• Volume of a Cylinder = $V = \pi r^2h$
• Curved Surface Area of a Cone = πrl
• Total Surface Area of a Cone = $\pi r(r + l) = \pi r[r + \sqrt{(h^2 + r^2)}]$
• Volume of a Cone = $V = ⅓ \times \pi r^2h$
• Surface Area of a Sphere = $S = 4\pi r^2$
• Volume of a Sphere = $V = 4/3 \times \pi r^3$
• Surface Area of a Cube = S = 6a2
Herein,
r denotes Radius,
h signifies Height, and
l represents Slant height.</td></tr>
<tr><td>Perimeter and Area</td><td>Perimeter of Square: 4a where a is the side of the square
Perimeter of Rectangle: 2(l + b) units, where l is length and b is the breadth
Area of Circle: πr^2 where r is the radius
Area of Rectangle: lb where l = length and b is the breadth
Total Surface Area (TSA) for Cube: $6a^2$
TSA of cuboid: 2(lb+bh+hl)</td></tr>
<tr><td>Exponents and Powers</td><td>$p^m \times p^n = p^{m+n}$
$\{p^m\}/\{p^n\} = p^{m-n}$
$(p^m)^n = p^{mn}$
$p^{-m} = 1/p^m$
$p^1 = p$
$p^0 = 1$</td></tr>
<tr><td>Representing 3D in 2D</td><td>Representing 3D objects in 2D drawings
1. Use plans from different viewpoints to represent 3D objects.
2. Draw isometric drawings of 3D objects.
3. Create nets for polyhedra (a three-dimensional solid with flat faces, straight edges, and sharp corners or vertices.)
4. Interpret the above representations to create a model of the 3D object.
❖ Formulas used in chapter: Practical Geometry</td></tr>
</table>

<table>
<tr><td>Constructions</td><td>1. Bisecting a Line Segment:
- To bisect a line segment AB, construct circles centered at A and B with the same radius greater than half the length of AB. The intersection of the two circles will give the midpoint of AB.
2. Constructing Perpendicular Lines:
- To construct a line perpendicular to a given line at a given point, use the following steps:
i. Place the compass at the given point and draw an arc that intersects the line on both sides.
ii. Without changing the compass width, place the compass at each point of intersection and draw arcs that intersect above and below the line.
iii. Connect the two points where the arcs intersect above and below the line. The line passing through the given point and the intersection points is perpendicular to the given line.
3. Constructing Parallel Lines:
- To construct a line parallel to a given line through a given point, use the following steps:
i. Place the compass at the given point and draw an arc that intersects the line at two points.
ii. Without changing the compass width, place the compass at each point of intersection and draw arcs above and below the line.
iii. Connect the points where the arcs intersect above and below the line. The line passing through the given point and the intersection points is parallel to the given line.
4. Constructing an Angle Bisector:
- To bisect an angle, use the following steps:
i. Place the compass at the vertex of the angle and draw an arc that intersects both rays of the angle.
ii. Without changing the compass width, place the compass at each point of intersection and draw arcs that intersect both rays of the angle.
iii. Connect the vertex of the angle with the point where the arcs intersect. The resulting line is the angle bisector.</td></tr>
<tr><td>Data Handling</td><td>The Average or Arithmetic Mean or Mean =
sum of observations / number of observations</td></tr>
</table>

CHAPTER- 1: INTEGERS

WORKSHEET - 1

1. **Fill in the blanks using < or >.**
   a. -2 …… -4
   b. 7 ……. -20
   c. -8 …… -2
   d. 5 …… -8

2. **Solve the following:**
   a. $(-6) \times (-5) + (-6)$
   b. $[(-6) \times (-3)] + (-3)$
   c. $(-10) \times [(-12) + (-10)]$
   d. $(-5) \times [(-6) + 5]$

3. **Using number line, find:**
   a. $4 \times (-5)$
   b. $6 \times (-2)$

4. **Solve the following:**
   a. $(-15) \times 8 + (-15) \times 4$
   b. $[32 + 2 \times 17 + (-6)] \div 15$

5. The sum of two integers is 116. If one of them is -79, find the other integers.

6. If a = -35, b = 10 cm and c = -5, verify that:
   a. $a + (b + c) = (a + b) + c$
   b. $a \times (b + c) = a \times b + a \times c$

7. **Write down a pair of integers whose**
   a. sum is -5
   b. difference is -7
   c. difference is -1
   d. sum is 0

8. You have ₹ 500 in your saving account at the beginning of the month. The record below shows all of your transactions during the month. How much money is in your account after these transactions?
   Amount in the beginning of the month in the account = ₹ 500
   Amount deposited in the account for Jal Board = ₹ 200
   Amount paid to Jal Board = ₹ 120
   Amount left in the account after the above transactions = ₹ (………. + ……… – ……..)
   = ₹ (……………. – ………………..) = ₹ …………………

   Amount deposited for LIC India = ₹ 150

Amount paid to LIC India = ₹ 240

Amount left after these transactions = ₹ (................. + ... – ....)

= ₹ (................ – ....) = ₹ ....

9. The given table shows the freezing points in °F of different gases at sea level. Convert each of these into °C to the nearest integral value using the relations and complete the table
C = 59 [F – 32]

Freezing point of Hydrogen = -435°F
C = ...
=
=
=

For Krypton, freezing point = -251°F
C ....
=
=
=

For Oxygen, freezing point = -369°F
C = ...
=
=
=

Hence, the required freezing points at sea level in °C for Hydrogen ....°C,
Krypton = ...°C, Oxygen = ...°C.

10. Write down the pair of integers whose:
    a. Sum is -4
    b. Sum is 0
    c. Difference is 2
    d. Difference is -6
11. Verify the following:
    a. (-22) × [(-4) + (-5)] = [(-22) × (-4)] + [(-22) × (-5)]
    b. (-12) × [(3) + (-9)] = [(-12) × (4)] + [(-12) × (-9)]
12. Evaluate
    a. (-100) ÷ 5
    b. (-36) ÷ (-4)
    c. ÷ (-12)
    d. [(-30) ÷ 5] ÷ 2
    e. (-40) ÷ 40

****

CHAPTER- 2: FRACTION AND DECIMALS

WORKSHEET - 2

*The word **fraction** is derived from the Latin word "**Fractus**" means broken. Represents the total component, which includes the number of equal parts out of a whole.*

Representation of Fractions

A fraction is represented by 2 more than one number, separated by a line.

Numerator / Denominator

Multiplying a fraction by a whole number:

Fraction multiplication by fraction is actually a numerical product / product of denominators.

1. MULTIPLE CHOICE :

i. If x= 9/11 and y= 4/15, then the value of x - y is

a. 5/165
b. 36/165
c. 91/165
d. 98/165

ii. Reciprocal of 7 is

a. -7
b. 1
c. 7
d. 1/7

iii. If the cost of 12 bananas is Rs 26.50, then the cost of 6 such bananas will be

a. Rs 10.50
b. Rs 12
c. Rs 13.25
d. Rs 20

iv. If the side of a square is 12.5 cm, then the area of square will be

a. 156.25 cm^2
b. 160 cm^2
c. 173.5 cm^2
d. 180 cm^2

v. Product of 0.04 x 1.1 is

a. 0.044

b. 0.44

c. 4.04

d. 4.4

vi. Decimal form of 15 rupees 5 paise is

a. Rs 15

b. Rs 15.5

c. Rs 155.0

d. Rs 15.05

vii. The value of 4kg 625g in gm will be

a. 4.620 g.

b. 4625 g

c. 40625 g

d. 400625 g

viii. If the length of a rectangle is 7.1 cm and its breadth is 2.5 cm, then the area of rectangle will :

a. 4.6 cm^2

b. 4.8 cm^2

c. 8.875 cm^2

d. 17.75 cm^2

ix. If a car covers a distance of 95.5 km in 2.5 hours, then the average distance covered by it in 1 hour will be

a. 38 km

b. 38.2 km

c. 38.3 km

d. 39 km

x. If we shift the decimal point two places towards right of a number 0.045, then the new number is

a. 0.0045

b. 4.5

c. 45

d. 450

2. How many 2/3 kg pieces can be cut from a cake of weight 4 kg?

3. What is the product of 5/129 and its reciprocal?

4. Sunita and Rehana want to make dresses for their dolls. Sunita has 3/4 m of cloth, and she gave 1/3 of it to Rehana. How much did Rehana have?

5. Anuradha can do a piece of work in 6 hours. What part of the work can she do in 1 hour, in 5 hours, in 6 hours?

6. **Multiply the following fractions.**

   a. $(\frac{2}{5}) \times 5\frac{1}{4}$
   b. $2\frac{3}{5} \times 3$

7. Divide 3/10 by (1/4 of 3/5).

8. **Evaluate the following:**

   i. $3\frac{1}{2} \div 4$
   ii. $4\frac{1}{3} \div 3$

9. 1/8 of a number equal 2/5 ÷ 1/20. What is the number?

10. Raj travels 360 km on three-fifths of his petrol tank. How far would he travel at the same rate with a full tank of petrol?

11. The product of two numbers is 2.0016. If one of them is 0.72, find the other number.

12. Write the place value of 3 in the following decimal numbers

    a. 3.65
    b. 32.97

13. **Express in kg .**

    a. 350 g
    b. 4120 g

14. Write the following decimal number is the expanded form.

    a. 30.13
    b. 321.5

15. Find

    a. 0.4 × 100
    b. 1.3 × 1000

16. Find

    a. 35.5 ÷ 10
    b. 235 ÷ 0.1

17. Udayan has brought 212kg tomatoes, 334 potatoes and 214kg of Brinjal from vegetable market. Find the total quantity of vegetables.

****

CHAPTER- 3: SIMPLE EQUATIONS & SIMPLE LINEAR EQUATIONS

WORKSHEET - 3

1. Write the following statements in the form of equations.

   (a) The sum of four times a number and 5 gives a number five times of it.
   (b) One-fourth of a number is 2 more than 5.

2. Convert the following equations in statement form:
   (a) $5x = 20$
   (b) $3y + 7 = 1$

3. If $k + 7 = 10$, find the value of $9k – 50$.

4. Solve the following equations:
   $3(y – 2) = 2(y – 1) – 3$

5. If 5 is added to twice a number, the result is 29. Find the number.

6. If one-third of a number exceeds its one-fourth by 1, find the number.

7. The length of a rectangle is twice its breadth. If its perimeter is 60 cm, find the length and the breadth of the rectangle.

8. Seven times a number is 12 less than thirteen times the same number. Find the number.

9. The present age of a son is half the present age of his father. Ten years ago, the father was thrice as old as his son. What is their present age?

10. The sum of three consecutive multiples of 2 is 18. Find the numbers.

11. Each of the 2 equal sides of an isosceles triangle is twice as large as the third side. If the perimeter of the triangle is 30 cm, find the length of each side of the triangle.

12. A man travelled two-fifth of his journey by train, one-third by bus, one-fourth by car and the remaining 3 km on foot. What is the length of his total journey?

13. Solve the following equations:

    a. $9m – 16 = 20$
    b. $-3(x + 2) = 12$
    c. $2y + 7\ 2 = 35\ 2$
    d. $5(2m – 2) =12$

13. Each of the 2 equal sides of an isosc
14.
15.
16. eles triangle is twice as large as the third side. If the perimeter of triangle is 30 cm. find the length of each equal sides of triangle.

15. The length of a rectangle is 3 units more than breadth and perimeter is 22 units. Find the length and breadth of the rectangle. 18. In a class of 35 students, the number of girls is two fifth of the number of boys. Find the number of girls and boys in the class.

16. Solve the following equation.

$$2(y - 5) + 3(y - 2) = 11 + 2(y - 3)$$

17. The angle of a triangle is in the ratio 2 : 3 : 4. Find all the three angles.

18. If $(y - 4)/5 = (y + 3)/5 + (y - 4)/3$, then find the value of y.

19. One fifth of a number is 5, then find the number.

20. If $y(y + 6) = y^2 + y + 25$, Find y.

21. Convert the following equations in statement form:

(i) $x - 5 = 9$

(ii) $5p = 20$

(iii) $3n + 7 = 1$

(iv) $\frac{m}{5} - 2 = 6$

22. Find a number, such that one-fourth of the number is 3 more than 7.

23. Solve the following equations:

$$3(y - 2) = 2(y - 1) - 3$$

24. Manu's father's age is 4 years more than three times Manu's age. Find Manu's age, if his father is 37 years old.

25. Solve:

a. $4(m + 3) = 18$
b. $-2(x + 3) = 8$

26. When you multiply a number by 6 and subtract 5 from the product, you get 7. Can you tell what the number is?

27. In a mathematics quiz, 30 prizes consisting 1st and 2nd are only to be given. 1st and 2nd prizes are worth Rs 2000 and Rs 1000 respectively. If the total prize money is Rs 52,000 then find the number of 1st prizes and 2nd prizes.

28. The length of a rectangle is twice its breadth. If its perimeter is 60 cm, find the length and the breadth of the rectangle.

29. The sum of three consecutive multiples of 2 is 18. Find the numbers.

30. Each of the 2 equal sides of an isosceles triangle is twice as large as the third side. If the perimeter of the triangle is 30 cm, find the length of each side of the triangle.

31. Solve:

    a. $3n + 7 = 25$
    b. $2p - 1 = 23$

32. Check whether the value given in brackets is solution to the given equation or not.

    a. $x - 7 = 17$ ($x = 10$)
    b. $y + 8 = 10$ ($y = 2$)

33. Raju's father's age is 5 years more than three times Raju's age. Find Raju's age, if his father is 44 years old.

34. Solve the following equation:

$$\frac{5z + 1}{3} = 7$$

35. Write equations for the following statements:

    a. 3 subtracted from 2 times of a number p is 9.
    b. Ten times a is 30.

36. If one-third of a number exceeds its one-fourth by 1, find the number.

37. Seven times a number is 12 less than thirteen times the same number. Find the number.

38. In a test, Abha gets twice the marks as that of Palak. Two times Abha's marks and three times Palak's marks make 280. Find Palak and Abha's marks.

39. If the interest received by Karim is Rs 30 more than that of Ramesh. If the total interest received by them is Rs 70, Find the interest received by Ramesh.

40. After 20 years, Manoj will be 5 times as old as he is now. Find his present age.

****

CHAPTER- 4: LINES AND ANGLES

WORKSHEET – 4

1. Find the angles which is 15 of its complement.
2. Find the angles which is 23 of its supplements.
3. Find the supplements of each of the following:

   (i) 30°

   (ii) 79°

   (iii) 179°

   (iv) x°

   (v) 25 of right angle
4. If the angles (4x + 4)° and (6x – 4)° are the supplementary angles, find the value of x.
5. Find the value of x. (6x – 40)° + (5x + 9)° + (3x + 15) ° = 180°
6. Find the value of y in the following figures:

   (i) y + 15° = 360°

   (ii) (2y + 10)° + 50° + 40° + 130° = 360°

   (iii) y + 90° = 180°
7. Two angles are equal and complement to each other. Find the equal angle.
8. Two angles are equal and supplement to each other. Find the equal angle.
9. Two supplementary angles are differed by 38°. Find the angles.
10. In the figure find a.

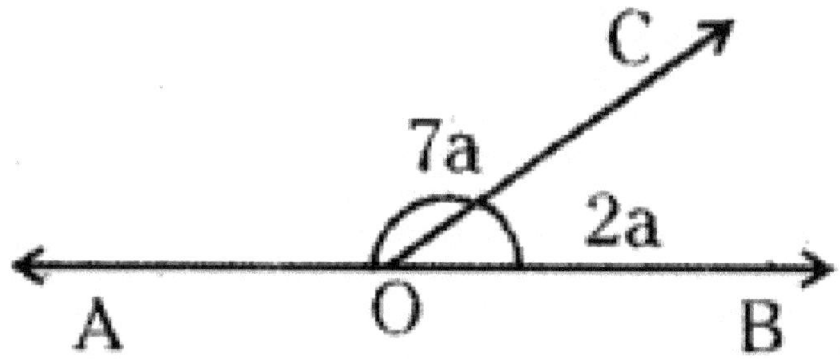

12. In the figure, find ∠x and ∠y.

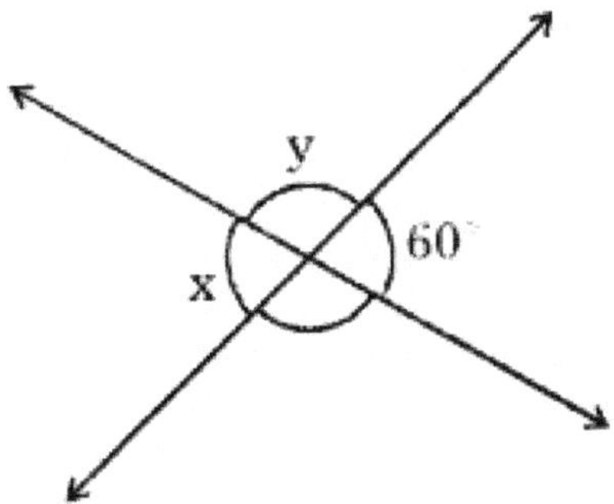

13. Write down each pair of adjacent angles in the figure.

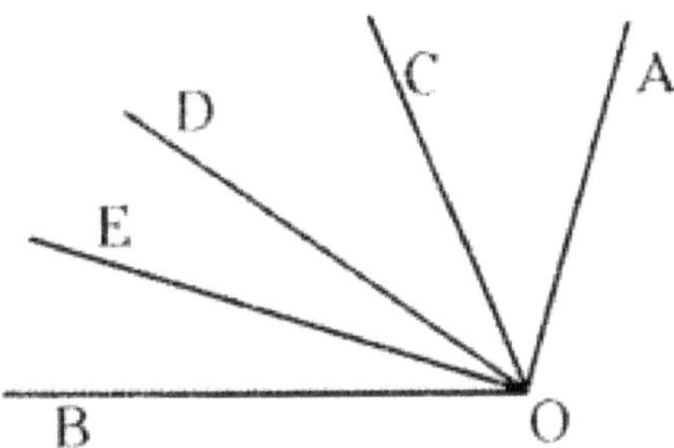

14. Find the complement of

    i) 73°,
    ii) 21°

15. Find the supplementary angle of

    i) 70°
    ii) 110°

16. Name all the pairs of adjacent angles.

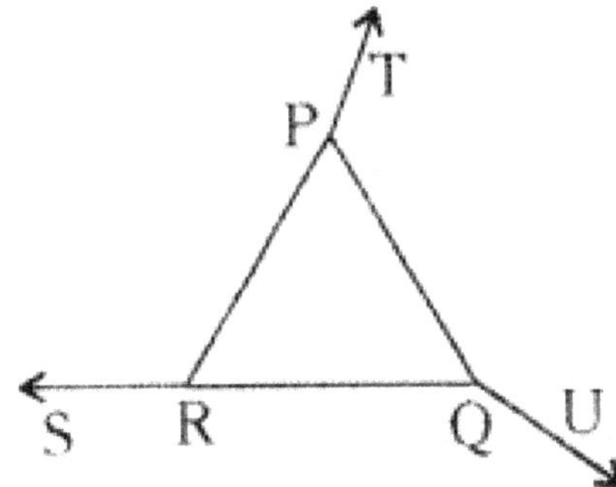

17. In the below figure what can you say about

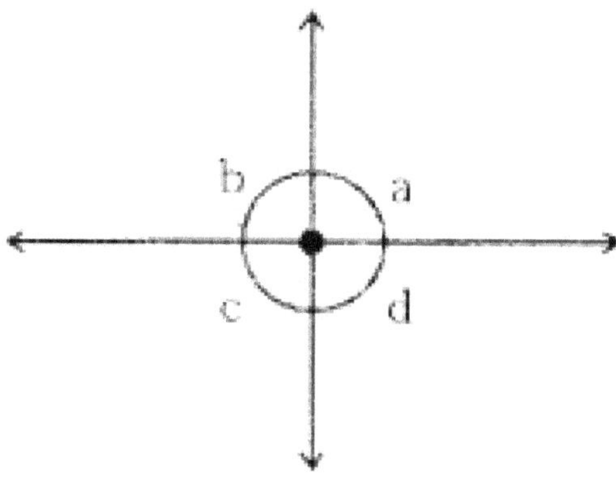

i)∠a + ∠b
ii)∠a + ∠b + ∠c + ∠d
ii) ∠c + ∠d = 180° (Linear pair)

18. In the below figure a : b = 2 : 3, then find a and b.

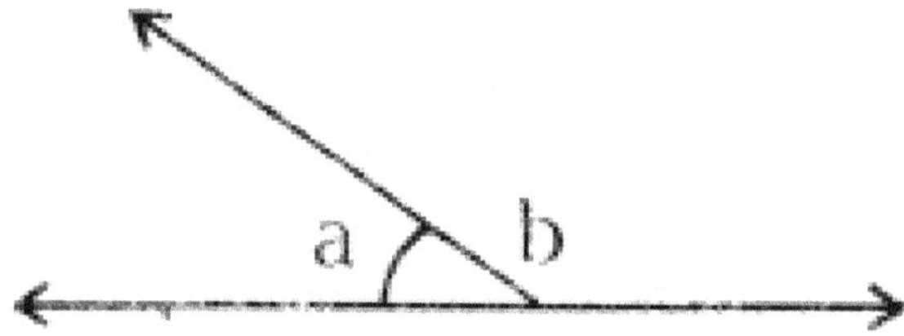

19. One of the angles of a linear pair is obtuse. What will be the other angle ?

20. Find x is the following figure.

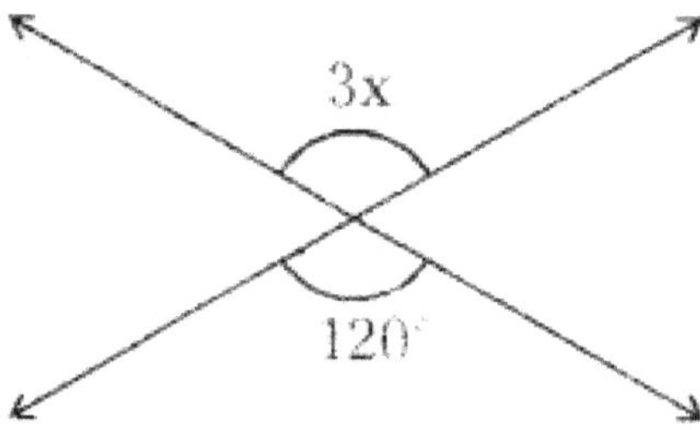

21. In the figure find 'a'.

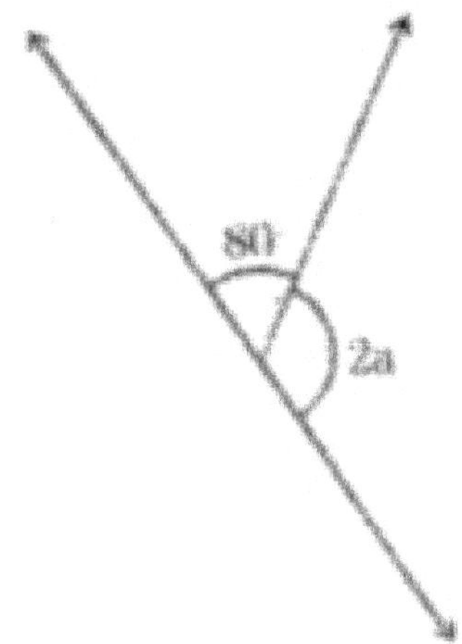

22. Draw
    i) a pair of intersecting lines
    ii) a pair of parallel lines

23. Find the value ∠1, ∠2 and ∠3, if ∠4 = 30°.

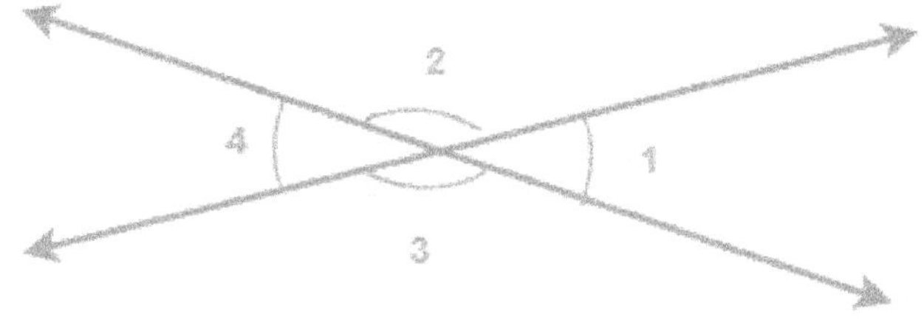

If p || q and r is transversal. Find the value ∠1, ∠2 and ∠3, if ∠4 = 110°.

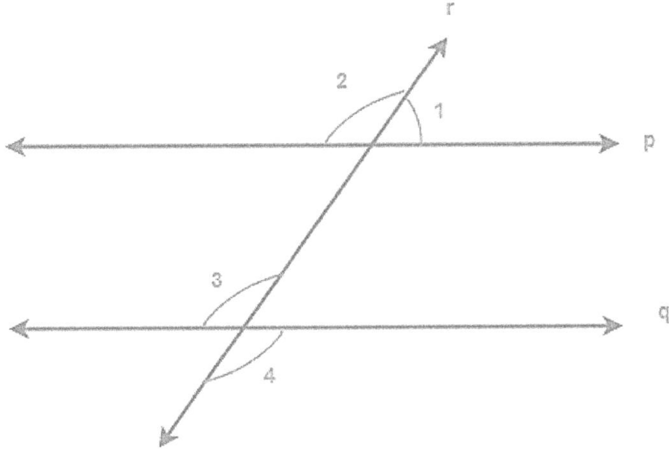

If p || q, ∠1 and ∠2 and are in the ratio of 2 : 3. Find angles ∠3, ∠4, ∠5, ∠6, ∠7 and ∠8.

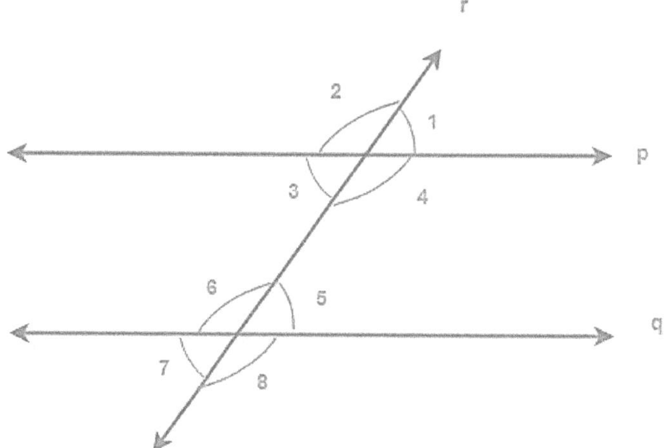

If AB || CD, find the values of x and y.

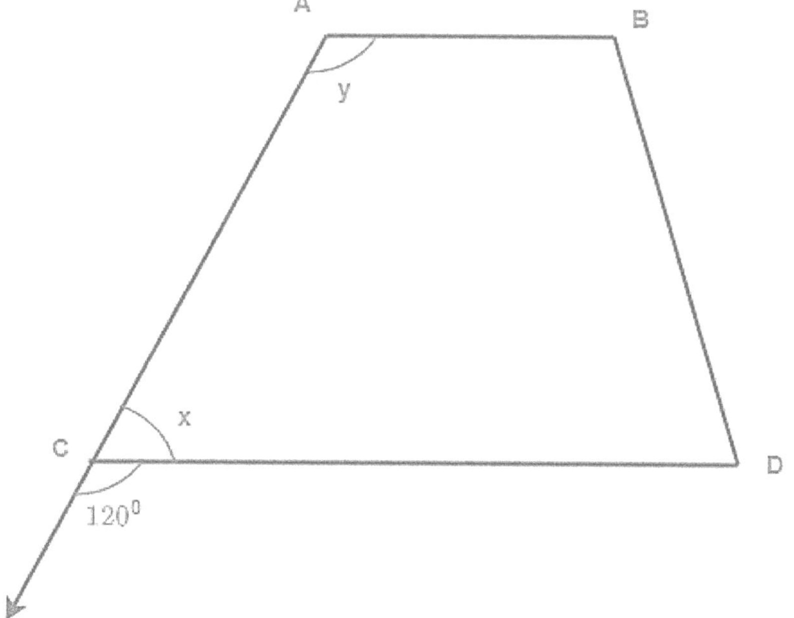

In the figure, p || q, r || s and ∠1 = 105°. Find the other angles.

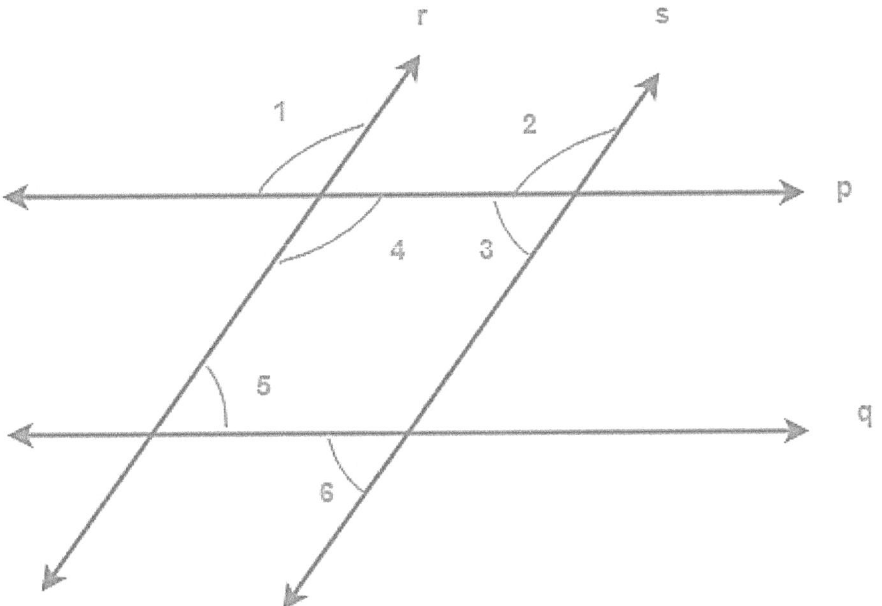

In the following figure FG || DE, ∠B = 30° and ∠C = 50°. Find values of x, y and z.

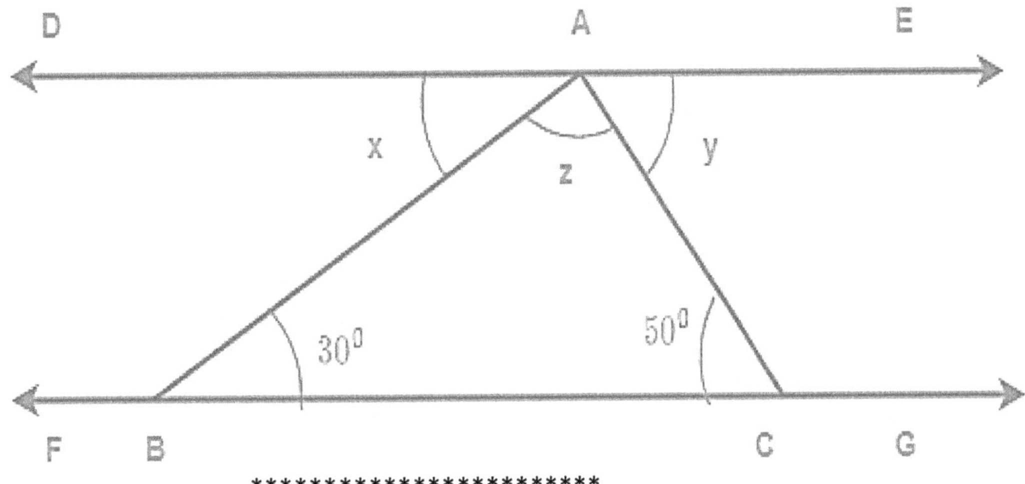

****

CHAPTER- 5: THE TRIANGLE AND ITS PROPERTIES

WORKSHEET – 5

1. Classify the following triangle on the bases of sides

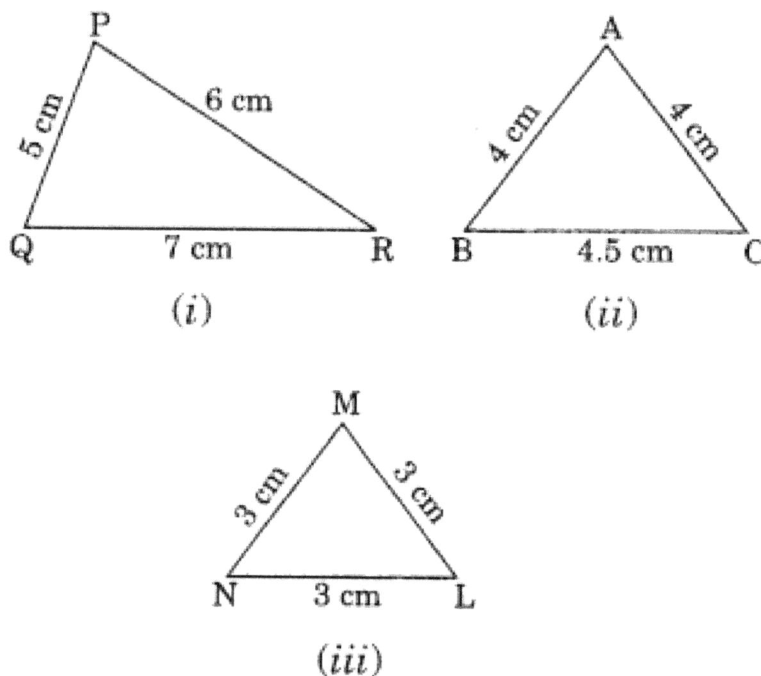

2. In a right-angled triangle, ΔABC, BC = 26 units and AB = 10 units. If BC is the longest side of the triangle, then what is the area of ΔABC?

3. In the given figure, name the median and the altitude. Here E is the midpoint of BC.

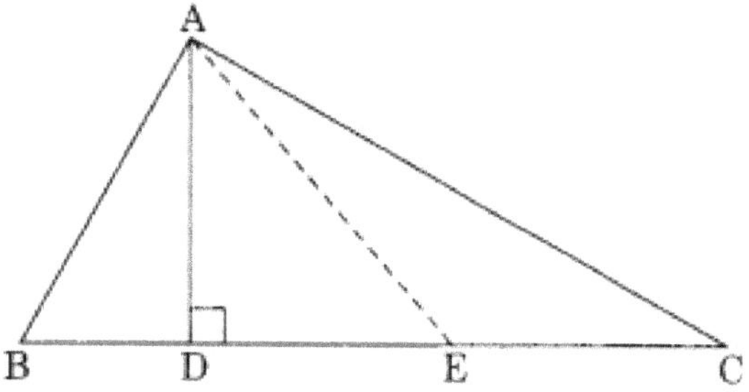

4. In an isosceles triangle DEF, if an interior angle ∠D = 100° then what is the value of ∠F?

5. In the given diagrams, find the value of x in each case.

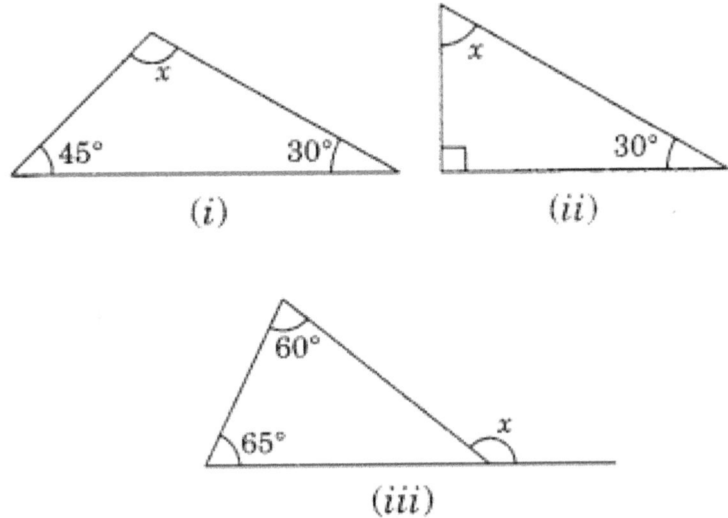

6. Which of the following cannot be the sides of a triangle?
   (i) 4.5 cm, 3.5 cm, 6.4 cm
   (ii) 2.5 cm, 3.5 cm, 6.0 cm
   (iii) 2.5 cm, 4.2 cm, 8 cm

7. In the given figure, find x.

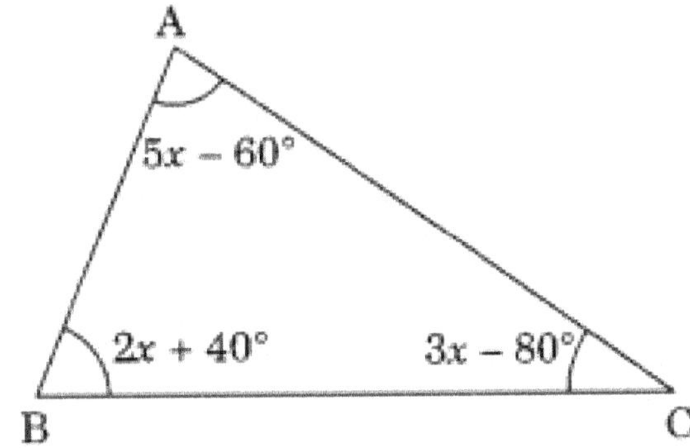

8. One of the equal angles of an isosceles triangle is 50°. Find all the angles of this triangle.

9. In ΔABC, $AC = BC$ and $\angle C = 110°$. Find $\angle A$ and $\angle B$.

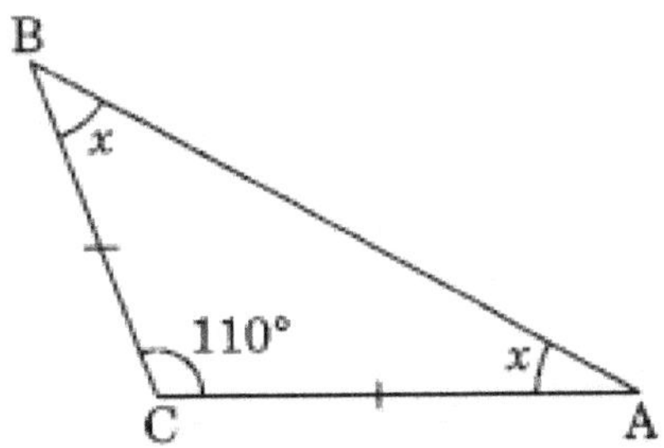

10. Two sides of a triangle are 4 cm and 7 cm. What can be the length of its third side to make the triangle possible?

11. Find whether the following triplets are Pythagorean or not?
(a) (5, 8, 17)
(b) (8, 15, 17)

12. In the given right-angled triangle ABC, ∠B = 90°. Find the value of x.

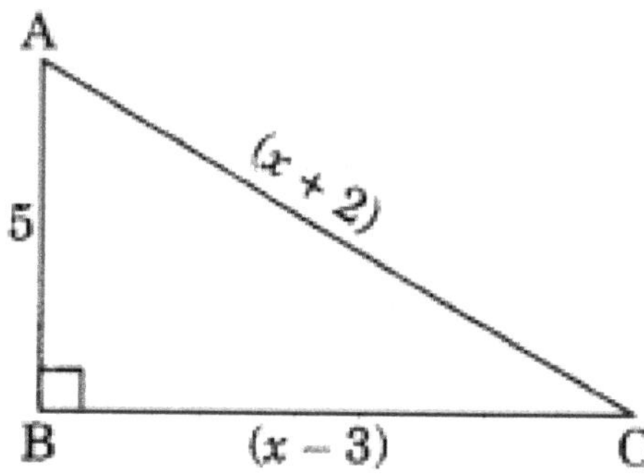

13. AD is the median of a ΔABC, prove that AB + BC + CA > 2AD.

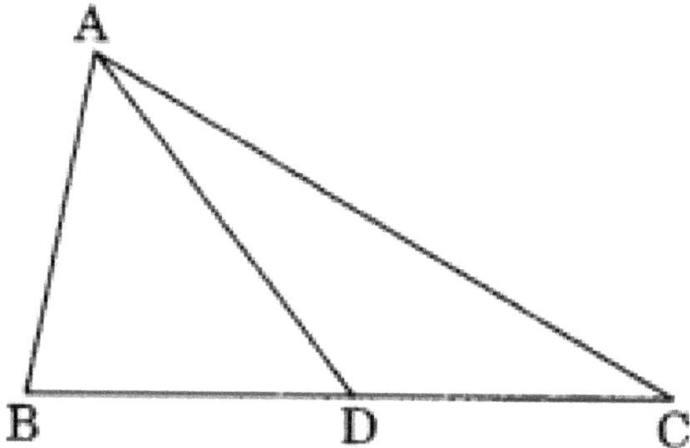

14. The length of the diagonals of a rhombus is 42 cm and 40 cm. Find the perimeter of the rhombus.

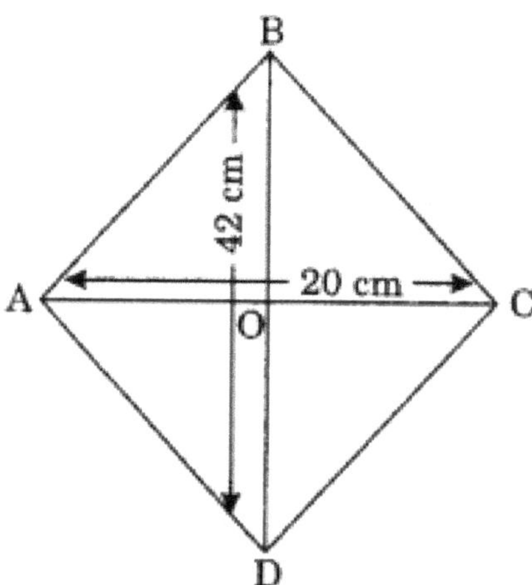

15. The sides of a triangle are in the ratio 3 : 4 : 5. State whether the triangle is right-angled or not.

16. A plane flies 320 km due west and then 240 km due north. Find the shortest distance covered by the plane to reach its original position.
(hint: diagram shown)

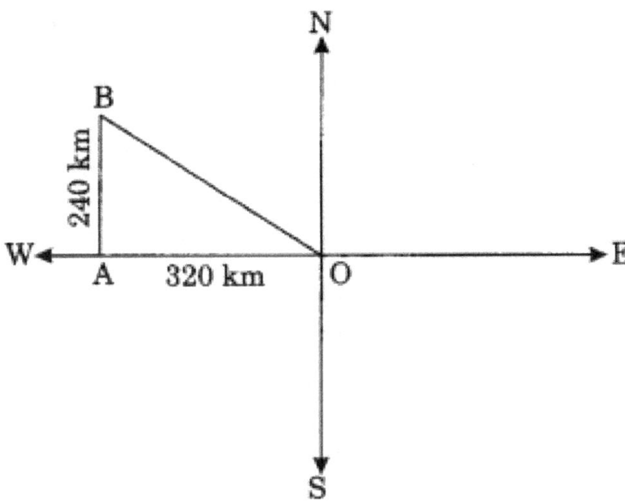

17. In the following figure, find the unknown angles a and b, if l || m.

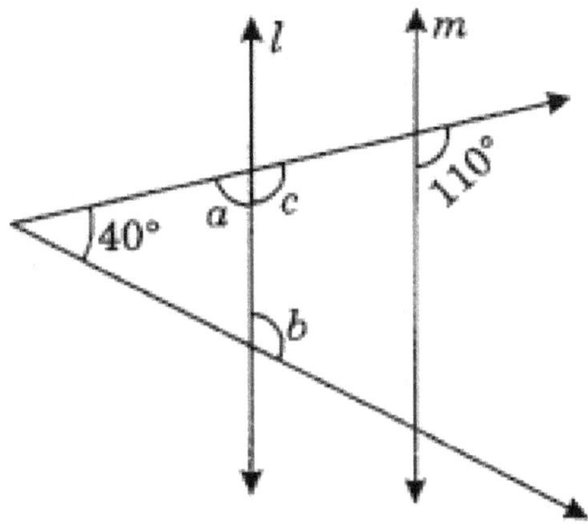

****

CHAPTER- 6: CONGRUENCE OF TRIANGLES

WORKSHEET - 6

1. **MCQ:**

i. If triangle ABC congruence to triangle CBD, then ∠ABC = ...

   a. ∠CDB
   b. ∠CBD
   c. ∠DCB

ii. Among two congruent angles, one has a measure of 60^0; the measure of the other angle is ....

   a. 50^0
   b. 70^0
   c. 60^0

iii. If you want to show two triangles are congruent, using the ASA rule then you need to show ....

   a. All angles are equal.
   b. All sides are equal.
   c. Two angle and 1 side are equal.

iv. What is the side included the angles M and N of MNP?

   a. MP
   b. NP
   c. MN

v. If you want to show two triangles are congruent, using the SAS rule then you need to show ....

   a. All angles are equal.
   b. Two angle and 1 side are equal.
   c. One angle and two sides are equal.

2. In the given figure, name

(a) the side opposite to vertex A
(b) the vertex opposite A to side AB
(c) the angle opposite to side AC
(d) the angle made by the sides CB and CA.

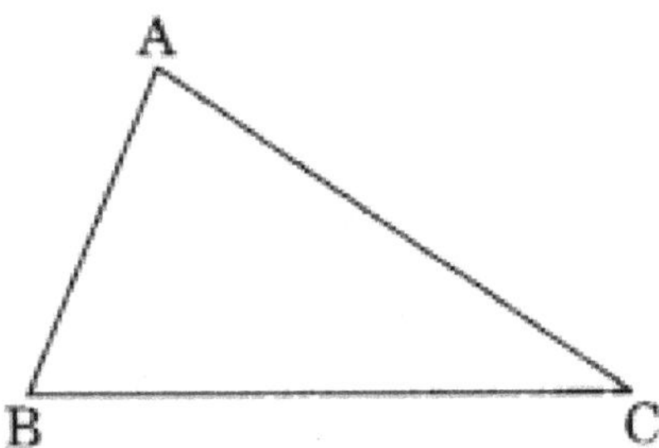

3. Examine whether the given triangles are congruent or not.

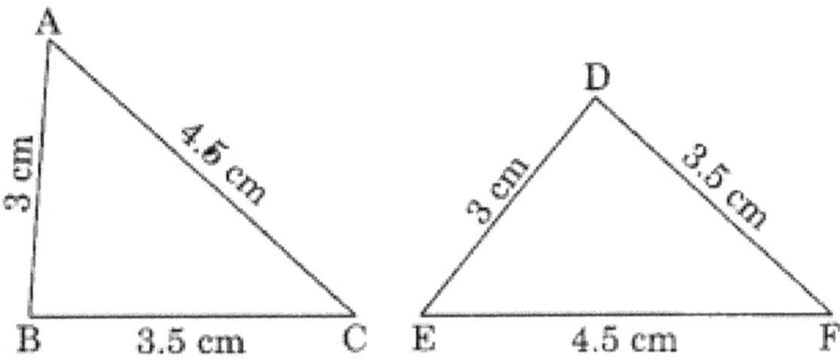

4. In the given congruent triangles under ASA, find the value of x and y, ΔPQR = ΔSTU.

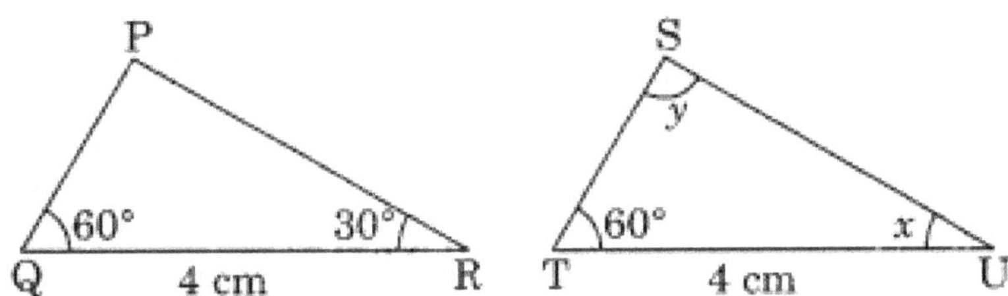

5. In the following figure, show that ΔPSQ = ΔPSR.

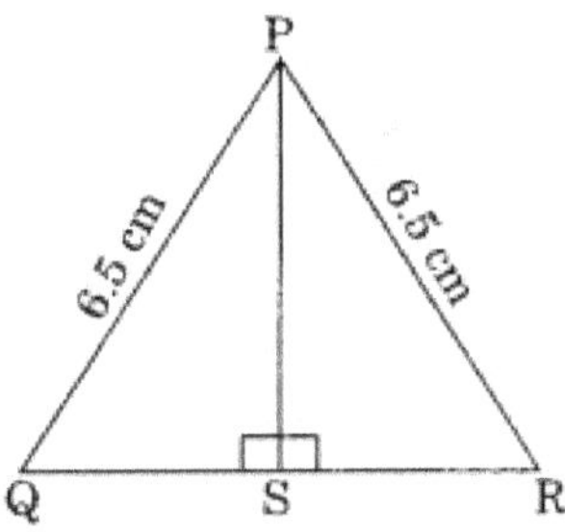

6. Can two equilateral triangles always be congruent? Give reasons.
7. In the given figure, AP = BQ, PR = QS. Show that ΔAPS = ΔBQR

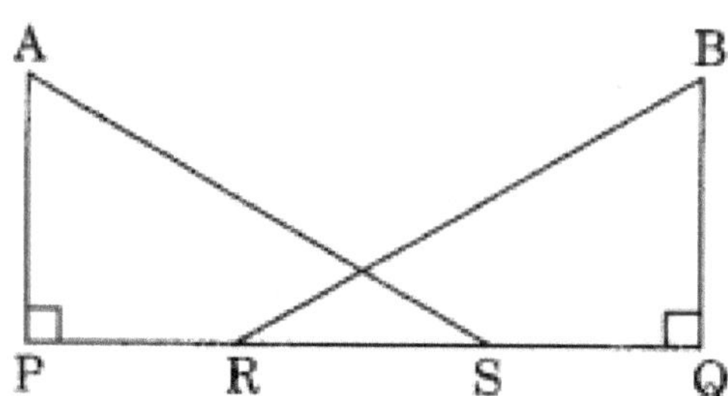

8. Without drawing the figures of the triangles, write all six pairs of equal measures in each of the following pairs of congruent triangles.
   (i) ΔABC = ADEF
   (ii) ΔXYZ = ΔMLN

   Lengths of two sides of an isosceles triangle are 5 cm and 8 cm, find the perimeter of the triangle.

   (Hint: 2 sides can be 5cm or 8cm) Solve both the case.

9. Write the rule of congruence in the following pairs of congruent triangles.

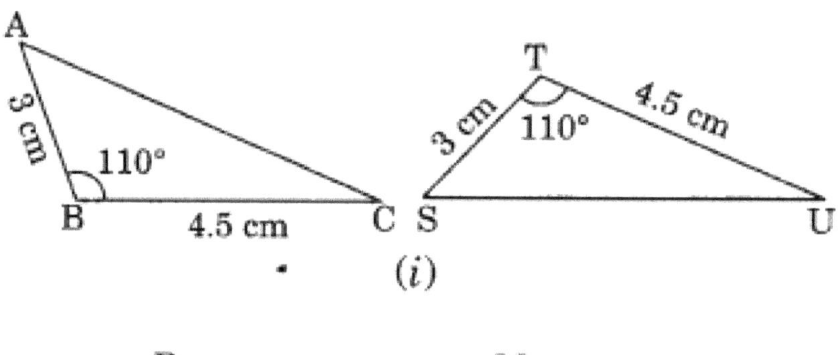

(i)

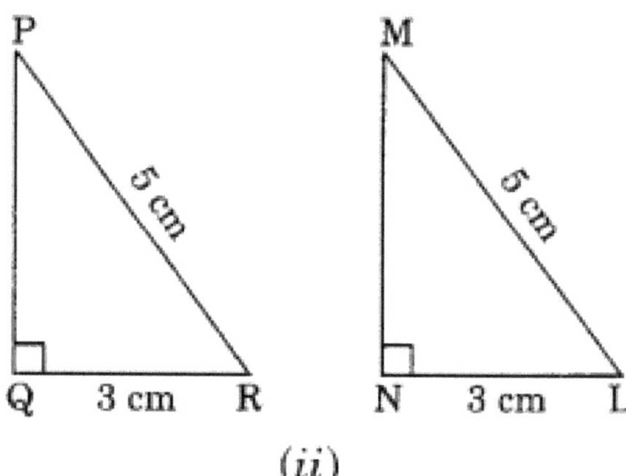

(ii)

10. In the given figure, state the rule of congruence followed by congruent triangles LMN and ONM.

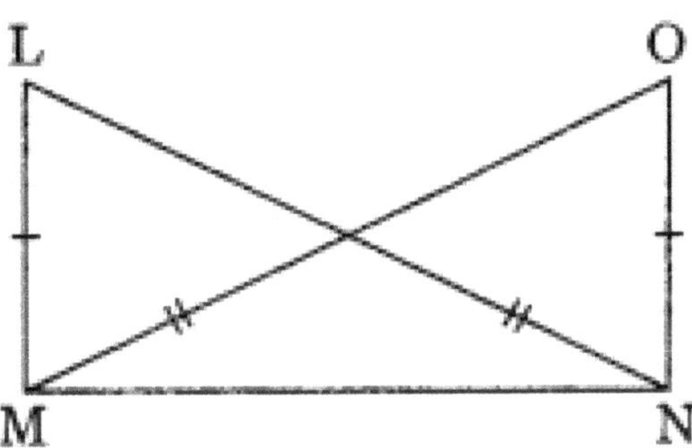

11. In the given figure, PQR is a triangle in which PQ = PR. QM and RN are the medians of the triangle. Prove that
(i) ΔNQR = ΔMRQ
(ii) QM = RN
(iii) ΔPMQ = ΔPNR

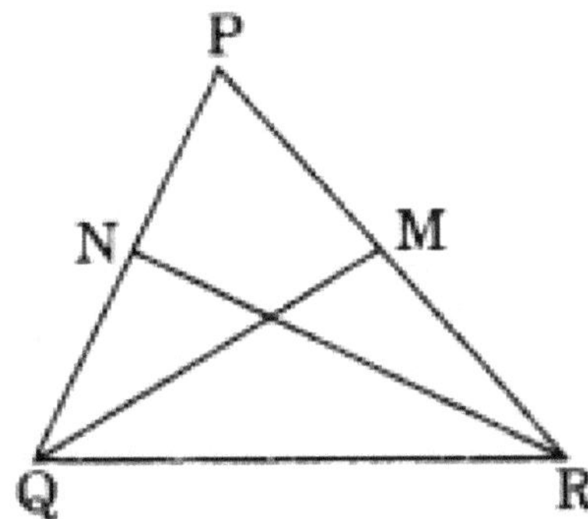

12. In the given figure, PQ = CB, PA = CR, ∠P = ∠C. Is ΔQPR = ΔBCA? If yes, state the criterion of congruence.

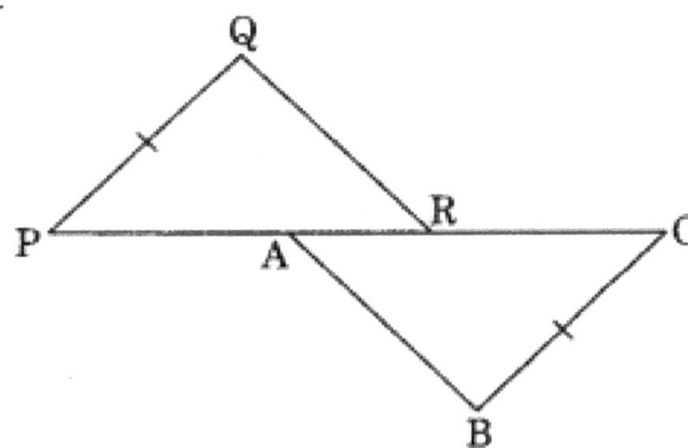

13. In the given figure, state whether ΔABC = ΔEOD or not. If yes, state the criterion of congruence.

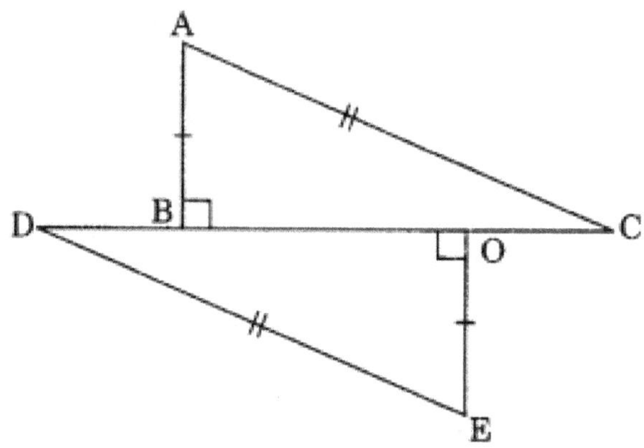

14. In the given figure, PQ || RS and PQ = RS. Prove that ΔPUQ = ΔSUR.

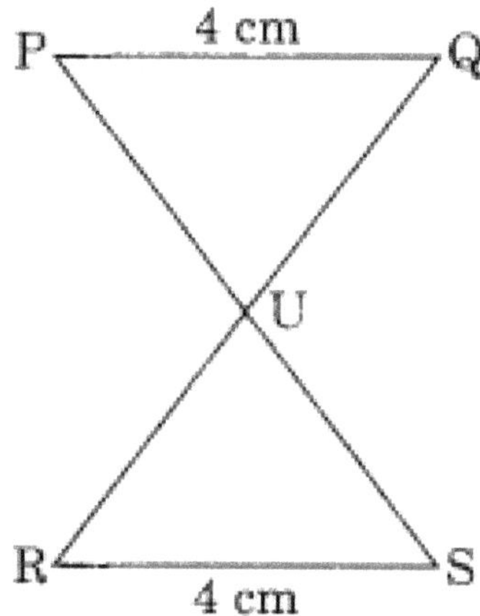

15. In the given figure ΔBAC = ΔQRP by SAS criterion of congruence. Find the value of x and y.

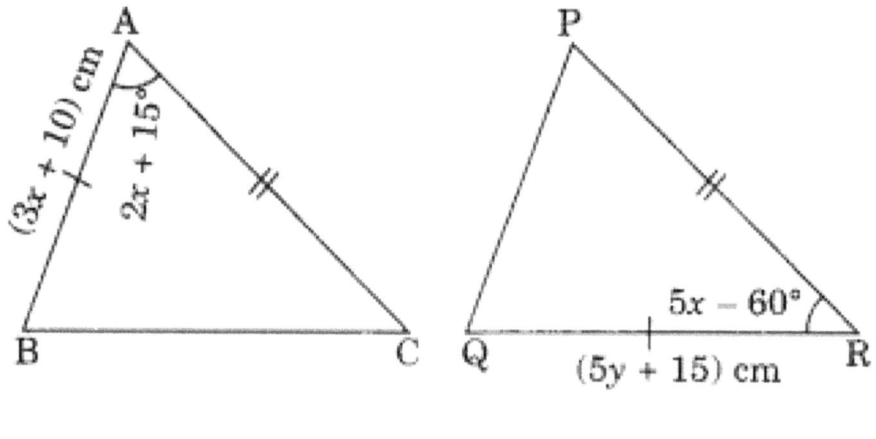

****

CHAPTER- 7: COMPARING QUANTITIES

WORKSHEET - 7

1. A shopkeeper bought 100 pencils for Rs. 250 and sold them for Rs. 300. What is the profit percentage?
2. A shopkeeper sells two fans at Rs. 2,000 each. If he makes a profit of 20% on one fan and a loss of 20% on the other, what is the overall profit or loss?
3. A shopkeeper bought 200 notebooks for Rs. 1,000 and sold them for Rs. 1,500. What is the profit percentage?
4. A shopkeeper sells two radios at Rs. 1,500 each. If he makes a profit of 10% on one radio and a loss of 10% on the other, what is the overall profit or loss?

5. A person borrowed Rs. 5,000 for 2 years at a simple interest rate of 5%. What is the amount of interest he has to pay?

6. The cost price of 15 pens is Rs. 120. What is the cost price of 20 pens?

7. A person borrowed Rs. 7,500 for 3 years at a simple interest rate of 6%. What is the amount of interest he has to pay?

8. A person borrowed Rs. 10,000 for 2 years at a simple interest rate of 4%. What is the amount of interest he has to pay?

9. A person borrowed Rs. 12,000 for 3 years at a simple interest rate of 5%. What is the amount of interest he has to pay?

10. The cost price of 20 pens is Rs. 160. What is the cost price of 25 pens?

11. If the price of a book increases by 10%, what is the new price of a book that originally cost Rs. 150?

12. If the price of a book decreases by 10%, what is the new price of a book that originally cost Rs. 200?

13. If the salary of a person increases by 15%, what is the new salary if his original salary was Rs. 12,000?

14. If 65% of students in class VII have a bicycle, then what is the percentage of the students who do not have bicycles ?

15. The cost of an object is increased by 12%. If the current cost is ₹ 896, what was its original cost?

16. In a furniture shop, 24 tables were bought at the rate of ₹ 450 per table. The shopkeeper sold 16 of them at the rate of ₹ 600 per table and the remaining at the rate of ₹ 400 per table. Find her gain or loss percent.

17. Mia obtains 480 marks out of 600. Shayan obtains 560 marks out of 700. Whose performance is better?

18. Rohan sells a sofa set for ₹ 9600 making a profit of 20%. What is the C.P. of the sofa set?

****

CHAPTER- 8: RATIONAL NUMBERS

WORKSHEET -8

1. **Write down the numerator of each of the following rational numbers:**

   a. (-17/-21)
   b. (8/9)
   c. 5

2. **Write down the denominator of each of the following rational numbers:**

   a. (-3/7)
   b. (11/-87)
   c. (-15/-42)
   d. 18
   e. 0

3. **Write down the rational number whose numerator is (-5) × 4, and whose denominator is (34 – 13) × (9 – 4).**

4. **Write down the rational numbers as integers: (3/1), (-52/1), (24/1), (-93/1), (65/1)**

5. **Write the following integers as rational numbers: -15, 17, 85, -100**

   (Hint: if no denominator is given means its 1)

6. **Write down the rational number whose numerator is the smallest three-digit number and denominator is the largest four-digit number.**

7. **Draw the number line and represent following rational number on it:**

   a. (1/3)
   b. (2/4)
   c. (5/8)
   d. (-5/8)
   e. (-3/16)
   f. (-8/3)
   g. (21/-7)
   h. (-13/3)

8. A rope is $\frac{7}{4}$ meters long. If it is cut into pieces of $\frac{1}{2}$ meter each, how many pieces are there?

9. A tank is $\frac{5}{6}$ full. If 10 liters of water are added to it, it becomes full. What is the capacity of the tank?

10. **Simplify:**

a. $^{2}/_{5} + ^{3}/_{10}$
b. $^{7}/_{8} - ^{1}/_{4}$
c. $^{3}/_{7} \times ^{4}/_{9}$
d. $^{5}/_{6} \div ^{2}/_{3}$

11. Express 24/36 in simplest form.

12. Convert 0.75 to a fraction and simplify.

13. Subtract 3/4 from 5/6.

14. Multiply 7/9 by 3/4.

15. Divide 8/15 by 2/5.

16. A cake recipe calls for 2/3 cup of sugar. If you want to make 1/2 of the recipe, how much sugar do you need?

17. Simplify the following expression: 3/4 + 1/6 – 1/3.

18. Find the value of 5/8 ÷ 2/3 × 4/5.

19. If 4/5 of a number is 20, what is the number?

20. Ravi has 7/12 of a liter of paint. He uses 1/3 of it to paint a wall. How much paint is left?

21. Find three rational numbers equivalent to each of the following rational numbers.

    (i) −25
    (ii) 37
    (Hint: -25 x 1, -25 x 2......)

22. Reduce the following rational numbers in standard form.

    (i) 35−15
    (ii) −36−216
    (Hint: convert to lowest form)

23. Represent 32 and −34 on number lines.

24. Which of the following rational numbers is greater?

    (i) 34, 12
    (ii) −32, −345.

25. If the product of two rational numbers is −916 and one of them is −415, find the other number.

26. Subtract the sum of −56 and -135 from the sum 223 and -625.

27. Divide the sum of -21517 and 3534 by their difference.

28. During a festival sale, the cost of an object is ₹ 870 on which 20% is off. The same object is available at other shops for ₹ 975 with a discount of 623 %. Which is a better deal and by how much?

29. Simplify:
$21.5 \div 5 - 15$ of $(20.5 - 5.5) + 0.5 \times 8.5$

30. Express 24/36 in simplest form.

31. Convert 0.75 to a fraction and simplify.

32. Subtract 3/4 from 5/6.

33. Multiply 7/9 by 3/4.

34. Divide 8/15 by 2/5.

35. A cake recipe calls for 2/3 cup of sugar. If you want to make 1/2 of the recipe, how much sugar do you need?

36. Simplify the following expression: 3/4 + 1/6 – 1/3.

37. Find the value of $5/8 \div 2/3 \times 4/5$.

38. If 4/5 of a number is 20, what is the number?

39. Ravi has 7/12 of a liter of paint. He uses 1/3 of it to paint a wall. How much paint is left?

40. Word Problems:

a) A rope is $\frac{7}{4}$ meters long. If it is cut into pieces of $\frac{1}{2}$ meter each, how many pieces are there?

b) A tank is $\frac{5}{6}$ full. If 10 liters of water are added to it, it becomes full. What is the capacity of the tank?

****

CHAPTER- 9: RATIO & PROPORTION

WORKSHEET - 9

1. Find the ratio of:

   (a) 5 km to 400 m
   (b) 2 hours to 160 minutes

2. State whether the following ratios are equivalent or not?

   (a) 2 : 3 and 4 : 5
   (b) 1 : 3 and 2 : 6
   (hint: LCM of 3 and 5, LCM of 3 & 6)

3. Express the following ratios in simplest form:

   (a) 615 : 213
   (b) 42 : 56

4. Compare the following ratios:

   3 : 4, 5 : 6 and 3 : 8

5. State whether the following ratios are proportional or not:

   (i) 20 : 45 and 4 : 9
   (ii) 9 : 27 and 33 : 11

6. 24, 36, x is in continued proportion, find the value of x.

7. Find the mean proportional between 9 and 16.

8. Find:

   (i) 36% of 400
   (ii) 1623% of 32

9. Find a number whose 614% is 12.

10. What per cent of 40 kg is 440 g?

11. Convert each of the following into the decimal form:

    (a) 25.2%
    (b) 0.15%
    (c) 25%

12. What per cent of

    (a) 64 is 148.48?
    (b) 75 is 1225?

Solution:

13. A machine costs ₹ 7500. Its value decreases by 5% every year due to usage. What will be its price after one year?

14. What sum of money lent out at 12 per cent p.a. simple interest would produce ₹ 9000 as interest in 2 years?

15. Rashmi obtains 480 marks out of 600. Rajan obtains 560 marks out of 700. Whose performance is better?

16. ₹ 9000 becomes ₹ 18000 at simple interest in 8 years. Find the rate per cent per annum.

17. The cost of an object is increased by 12%. If the current cost is ₹ 896, what was its original cost?

18. Radhika borrowed ₹ 12000 from her friends. Out of which ₹ 4000 were borrowed at 18% and the remaining at 15% rate of interest per annum. What is the total interest after 3 years?

19. Rajan's monthly income is 20% more than the monthly income of Sarita. What per cent of Sarita's income is less than Rajan's monthly income?

20. If 10 apples are bought for ₹ 11 and sold at the rate of 11 apples for ₹ 10. Find the overall gain or loss per cent in these transactions.

21. If 25 men can do a work in 36 hours, find the number of men required to do the same work in 108 hours.

22. A machine is sold by A to B at a profit of 10% and then B sold it to C at a profit of 20%. If C paid ₹ 1200 for the machine, what amount was paid by A to purchase the machine?

23. Are the two ratios 8:10 and 7:10 in proportion?

24. The earnings of Rohan are 12000 rupees every month and Anish is 191520 per year. If the monthly expenses of every person are around 9960 rupees. Find the ratio of the savings.

25. Twenty tons of iron is Rs. 600000 (six lakhs). What is the cost of 560 kilograms of iron?

26. The dimensions of the rectangular field are given. The length and breadth of the rectangular field are 50 meters and 15 meters. What is the ratio of the length and breadth of the field?

27. Obtain a ratio of 90 centimeters to 1.5 meters.

28. There exists 45 people in an office. Out of which female employees are 25 and the remaining are male employees. Find the ratio of

    a] The count of females to males.

    b] The count of males to females.

29. Write two equivalent ratios of 6: 4.

30. Out of the total students in a class, if the number of boys is 5 and the number of girls is 3, then find the ratio between girls and boys.

31. Two numbers are in the ratio 2 : 3. If the sum of numbers is 60, find the numbers.

32. Compare the following ratios.

(a) 5 : 7 and 4 : 3

(b) 1/3 : 1/4 and 1/5 : 1/4

(c) $2\frac{1}{2}$: $3\frac{1}{3}$ and 0.3 : 1

33. Determine if the following ratios form a proportion.

(a) 32 m : 64 m = 7 seconds : 14 seconds

(b) 6.5 litres : 13 litres = 50 kg : 10 kg

34. Find the fourth proportional to

(a) 5.6, 2.1, 1.6, x

(b) 3/4, 15/16, 2/4, x

(c) $5\frac{3}{5}$, $3\frac{1}{2}$, 2, x

(d) 8, 6, 4, x

35. **Find the third proportional to**

(a) 9, 6, x

(b) 0.2, 0.4, x

(c) 9/16, 3/5, x

(d) 6, 12, x

36. The number of male and female in an office are 520 and 650 respectively. Find the ratio of female to the total number of employees.

37. Two number are in the ratio 5 : 7. If sum of the numbers is 840, find them.

38. The length of a swimming pool is 26 m and its breadth is 15.6 m. Find the ratio of its length to its breadth.

39. If 30 bed covers cost Rs. 70, what is the cost of 6 dozen bed covers?

40. 23 kg of sugar costs Rs. 333.50. What is the cost of 12 kg sugar?

41. A web designer earned Rs. 53200 in 28 months. How much does he earn in 6 months?

42. If a dozen of eggs costs Rs. 90.84, how many eggs can be bought for Rs. 166.54?

43. Find x in the following proportions

(i) 6 : 15 = 2 : x

(ii) 2 : 4 = x : 10

(iii) x : 3 = 8 : 12

44. If the cost of 17 metres carpet is Rs. 340, find the cost of 11 metres.

45 Alexander can type 2820 words in one hour. How many words can he type in 15 minutes?

****

CHAPTER- 10 :ALGEBRAIC EXPRESSIONS

WORKSHEET - 10

1. MCQ:

i. $7a - 4(a^2 + b^2)$ is a __________ expression.
a) Monomial b) Binomial
c) Trinomial d) None of these

ii. The coefficient of 3p in $-3p^3qr$ is _____.
a) p^3qr b) $-p^3qr$
c) p^2qr d) $-p^2qr$

iii. 14. If a = 5, b = −1, then a^{-b} = _____.
a) 5 b) 1
c) 0 d) −5

iv. If p = 3, q = −4, then q^p = _____.
a) 64 b) −64
c) 46 d) None of these

v. The perimeter of triangle having sides as 3p, 2q and (p + q) is _____.
a) 3p + 2q b) 3p − 2q
c) 4p + 3q d) None of these

vi. Find the degree of the given polynomial: $5a^2 + 2ab^2 + 7$
a) 0 b) 1
c) 2 d) 3

vii. Find the value of the algebraic expression $3p^3 + 2p^2 - 7p + 5$ when p = −1.
a) 14 b) 11
c) 17 d) None of these

viii. If length and breadth of a rectangle are 2x + y and x + y, then find its perimeter.
a) 4x + 2y b) 6x − 4y
c) 6x + 4y d) 6x + 6y

ix. Numerical coefficient of $-5a^2b$ is _____.
a) 5 b) a^2b
c) -5 d) $-5a^2$

2. Simplify the following expressions:

i. 5x + 3x − 2x

ii. $7y - 4y + 9$

iii. $3a + 4a - 5 + 2$

3. **Identify the coefficients in the following algebraic expressions:**

i. $7x + 9$

ii. $3m - 5n + 2$

iii. $-4p + 6q - 3$

4. **Form an algebraic expression for the following statements:**

i. The sum of three times a number x and 11.

ii. The product of 5 and the difference of a number y and 4.

iii. Twice the sum of a number z and 3.

5. **Add the following algebraic expressions:**

i. $2x + 5y$ and $3x - 4y$

ii. $7a - 3b + 2$ and $4a + 5b - 6$

iii. $x + 2y - 3z$ and $-x + y + 4z$

6. **Subtract the second expression from the first:**

i. $6m + 9n$ from $12m - 5n$

ii. $3p - 4q + 2$ from $7p + 6q - 3$

iii. $x - 2y + 3z$ from $4x + y - z$

7. Multiply the following expressions:

i. $2x (3x + 5)$

ii. $-4y (y - 7)$

iii. $5 (2a - 3b + 4)$

7. If $a = 2$, $b = -3$, and $c = 4$, find the value of the following expression:

i. $3a + 2b - c$

ii. $5a - 4b + 2c$

8. Simplify the expression and then find its value when $x = 3$ and $y = -2$:

$4x - 5y + 6$

9. Add the below mentioned algebraic expressions.

$5p + 7q - 12r$
$15r + 3q + 2p$

10. Add the below mentioned algebraic expressions.

$5p^3 + 3p^2 + 10p$
$-2p^3 - 2p^2 + 5p$

11. Subtract $2p - 3q + 4r$ from $5p + 3q - 2r$.

12. Subtract $2a^2 - 3a + 4$ from $5a^2 + 6a - 2$.

13. If $a = -3$, $b = -4$, then find the value of $3(a^2 + ab) + 3 - 2ab$.

14. When $a = 2$, $b = -1$, $c = -2$, then find the values of $a^3 + b^3 + c^3 + 3abc$.

15. Write the degree of following polynomials.

$\frac{3}{5}ab^2 + 4ab + \frac{2}{3}a^2b^2 + 5b$

16. How much is $5a^2 - 7ab + 4b^2 + 6$ greater than $3a^2 + 2ab + 4$?

17. What must be added $5p^3 - 3p^2 + 4p + 3$ to get $8p^3 + 6p - 7$?

18. Simplify: $75 - [12y - 5(3y - 2) - 2\{12y - 2(2 - 4y)\}]$

19. From the sum of $5a + 2$ and $5a^2 + 7a - 4$ subtract the sum of $3a^2 - 5a$ and $4a - 5a^2 + 7$.

20. What should be deducted from $3p^2 - 5q^2 + 8pq + 25$ to get $p^2 + 4q^2 + 6pq + 20$.

****

CHAPTER- 11:PERCENTAGE AND ITS APPLICATIONS

WORKSHEET - 11

1. Express each of the following percent (%):

(i) 3/5

(ii) $1^1/_2$

(iii) 3/10

(iv) 13/20

(v) 0.86

(vi) 0.73

(vii) 3.28

(viii) 1.073

2. In each case, given below, express the second quantity as the percent of the first:

(i) 5, 4

(ii) 4, 5

(iii) 5 m, 80m

(iv) 0.8, 0.6

(v) 3, 1.8

(vi) 1.8, 1.35

3. Find the resulting (increased or decreased) quantity due to:

(i) 15 % increase in 38 kg

(ii) $12^1/_2$% increase in Rs. 450

(iii) $7^1/_3$ % decrease in 36

4. Mr. Sharma has a monthly salary of Rs. 7, 500. If he spends Rs. 6,250 every month, find his expenditure and savings in percent?

5. In a school there are 1500 boys and some are girls. If the number of boys is 75 %, calculate the number of girls.

6. A man bought an old car and spent 20 % of the cost of repairs. If his total cost including repairs was Rs. 1,20,000, at what price did he buy the car?

7. The total capacity of a tank is 200 litres. At present it is 60 % full with water. Some water is taken from the tank and it is found that the tank is now 35 % full. Find the quantity of water taken.

8. In a mixture of two liquids A and B: 35 % is liquid B. If the total quantity of the mixture is 20 kg; find the quantity of A, by weight, in the mixture.

9. The price of an article increased from Rs. 16 to Rs. 20; find the percentage increase.

10. After an increase of 20 %; a number becomes 540. Find the original number.

11. Mr. Mohan saves 33 % of his income, what percent of his income does he spend?

12. There are 250 students in grade V. Out of these 100 are girls. What percent of students are girls? What percent of students are boys?

13. David read 150 pages of a book. If the book contains 200 pages, what percent of the book has David read?

14. 20% of the trees in an orchard are orange trees. If there are 50 orange trees, what is the total number of trees in the orchard?

15. Find the amount received on Rs 4000 for 2 years at the rate of 11% per annum?

16. What is the percentage increase when 284 is increased to 320?

17. At what rate of interest will Rs 350 amount to Rs 455 in 6 years?

18. The price of a book is Rs 350. If there is an increase of 10% in the price, what will be the new price of the book?

19. If Rs 250 amounts to Rs 285 in 2 years , find the rate of interest per annum.

20. A man weighed 80 kg. After he had joined a fitness Centre , he weighed 58 .By what percent did his weight reduce?

****

CHAPTER- 12: PRACTICAL GEOMETRY

WORKSHEET - 12

1. State whether the triangle is possible to construct if

   (a) In ΔABC, m∠A = 80°, m∠B = 60°, AB = 5.5 cm
   (b) In ΔPQR, PQ = 5 cm, QR = 3 cm, PR = 8.8 cm

2. Draw an equilateral triangle whose each side is 4.5 cm.
3. Draw a ΔPQR, in which QR = 3.5 cm, m∠Q = 40°, m∠R = 60°.
4. There are four options, out of which one is correct. Choose the correct one:

   (i) A triangle can be constructed with the given measurement.

   (a) 1.5 cm, 3.5 cm, 4.5 cm
   (b) 6.5 cm, 7.5 cm, 15 cm
   (c) 3.2 cm, 2.3 cm, 5.5 cm
   (d) 2 cm, 3 cm, 6 cm

   (ii) (a) m∠P = 40°, m∠Q = 60°, AQ = 4 cm

   (b) m∠B = 90°, m∠C = 120° , AC = 6.5 cm
   (c) m∠L = 150°, m∠N = 70°, MN = 3.5 cm
   (d) m∠P = 105°, m∠Q = 80°, PQ = 3 cm

5. What will be the other angles of a right-angled isosceles triangle?
6. What is the measure of an exterior angle of an equilateral triangle?
7. In ΔABC, ∠A = ∠B = 50°. Name the pair of sides which are equal.
8. If one of the other angles of a right-angled triangle is obtuse, whether the triangle is possible

   to construct.
9. State whether the given pair of triangles are congruent.
10. Draw a ΔABC in which BC = 5 cm, AB = 4 cm and m∠B = 50°.
11. Draw ΔPQR in which QR = 5.4 cm, ∠Q = 40° and PR = 6.2 cm.
12. Construct a ΔPQR in which m∠P = 60° and m∠Q = 30°, QR = 4.8 cm.
13. Draw an isosceles right-angled triangle whose hypotenuse is 5.8 cm.
14. Construct a ΔABC such that AB = 6.5 cm, AC = 5 cm and the altitude AP to BC is 4 cm.
15. Construct an equilateral triangle whose altitude is 4.5 cm.
16. Fill in the blanks:

   (i) A triangle can be drawn if the _____ and a leg in the case of a right-angled triangle.
   (ii) We can draw ____________ line (s) parallel to a given line.
   (iii) The number of line (s) that can be drawn parallel to a given line through a given

point not on the line is ________________.

(iv) A triangle can be drawn only when the sum of any two sides of the triangle is _______________ than third side.

(v) Construction of a triangle is not possible if three ________________ of a triangle are given.

(vi) The sum of angles of a triangle is ______________ right angles.

(vii) A triangle can be drawn if _____ sides and one angle given.

(viii) A triangle in which all three sides are of equal lengths is called _________.

****

CHAPTER- 13: PERIMETER AND AREA

WORKSHEET - 13

1. The side of a square is 2.5 cm. Find its perimeter and area.

2. If the perimeter of a square is 24 cm. Find its area.

3. If the length and breadth of a rectangle are 36 cm and 24 cm respectively. Find

   (i) Perimeter
   (ii) Area of the rectangle.

4. The perimeter of a rectangular field is 240 m. If its length is 90 m, find:

   (i) it's breadth
   (ii) it's area.

5. The length and breadth of a rectangular field are equal to 600 m and 400 m respectively. Find the cost of the grass to be planted in it at the rate of ₹ 2.50 per m^2.

6. The perimeter of a circle is 176 cm, find its radius.

7. The radius of a circle is 3.5 cm, find its circumference and area.

8. Area of a circle is 154 cm^2, find its circumference.

9. The length of the diagonal of a square is 50 cm, find the perimeter of the square.

10. A wire of length 176 cm is first bent into a square and then into a circle. Which one will have more area?

11. A rectangle park is 45 m long and 30 m wide. A path 2.5 m wide is constructed outside the park. Find the area of the path.

12. Question 16.
    How many times a wheel of radius 28 cm must rotate to cover a distance of 352 m?
    (Take π = 227) (Hint: circumference = $2\pi r$. Distance covered- change to cm / $2\pi r$)

13. Find the area of a parallelogram-shaped shaded region. Also, find the area of each triangle. What is the ratio of the area of shaded portion to the remaining area of the rectangle?

14. Find the area of the following polygon if AB = 12 cm, AC = 2.4 cm, CE = 6 cm, AD = 4.8 cm, CF = GE = 3.6 cm, DH = 2.4 cm.

15. Identify in the given expressions, terms which are not constants. Give their numerical coefficients.

    (i) $5x - 3$
    (ii) $11 - 2y^2$
    (iii) $2x - 1$

(iv) $4x^2y + 3xy^2 - 5$

16. Group the like terms together from the following expressions:

$-8x^2y$, $3x$, $4y$, $-32x$, $2x^2y$, $-y$

17. Identify the pairs of like and unlike terms:

(i) $-32x$, y
(ii) $-x$, $3x$
(iii) $-12y2x$, $32xy^2$
(iv) 1000, -2

18. Classify the following into monomials, binomial and trinomials.

(i) -6
(ii) $-5 + x$
(iii) $32x - y$
(iv) $6x^2 + 5x - 3$
(v) $z^2 + 2$

19. Draw the tree diagram for the given expressions:

(i) $-3xy + 10$
(ii) $x^2 + y^2$

20. Identify the constant terms in the following expressions:

(i) $-3 + 32x$
(ii) $32 - 5y + y^2$
(iii) $3x^2 + 2y - 1$

21. Add:

(i) $3x^2y$, $-5x^2y$, $-x^2y$
(ii) $a + b - 3$, $b + 2a - 1$

22. Subtract $3x^2 - x$ from $5x - x^2$.

23. Simplify combining the like terms:

(i) $a - (a - b) - b - (b - a)$
(ii) $x^2 - 3x + y^2 - x - 2y^2$

24. Subtract $24xy - 10y - 18x$ from $30xy + 12y - 14x$.
25. From the sum of $2x^2 + 3xy - 5$ and $7 + 2xy - x^2$ subtract $3xy + x^2 - 2$.
26. Subtract $3x^2 - 5y - 2$ from $5y - 3x^2 + xy$ and find the value of the result if $x = 2$, $y = -1$.
27. Simplify the following expressions and then find the numerical values for $x = -2$.

(i) $3(2x - 4) + x^2 + 5$
(ii) $-2(-3x + 5) - 2(x + 4)$

28. Find the value of t if the value of $3x^2 + 5x - 2t$ equals to 8, when $x = -1$.

29. Subtract the sum of $-3x^3y^2 + 2x^2y^3$ and $-3x^2y^3 - 5y^4$ from $x^4 + x^3y^2 + x^2y^3 + y^4$.

30. What should be subtracted from $2x^3 - 3x^2y + 2xy^2 + 3y^2$ to get $x^3 - 2x^2y + 3xy^2 + 4y^2$?

31. To what expression must $99x^3 - 33x^2 - 13x - 41$ be added to make the sum zero?

32. If $P = 2x^2 - 5x + 2$, $Q = 5x^2 + 6x - 3$ and $R = 3x^2 - x - 1$. Find the value of $2P - Q + 3R$.

33. If $A = -(2x + 3)$, $B = -3(x - 2)$ and $C = -2x + 7$. Find the value of k if $(A + B + C) = kx$.

34. Rohan's mother gave him ₹ $3xy^2$ and his father gave him ₹ $5(xy^2 + 2)$. Out of this total money he spent ₹ $(10 - 3xy^2)$ on his birthday party. How much money is left with him?

****

CHAPTER- 14: EXPONENTS AND POWERS

WORKSHEET - 14

1. Express 343 as a power of 7.

2. Which is greater 3^2 or 2^3?

3. Express the following number as a power of prime factors:

   (i) 144
   (ii) 225

4. Find the value of:

   (i) $(-1)^{1000}$
   (ii) $(1)^{250}$
   (iii) $(-1)^{121}$
   (iv) $(10000)^0$

5. Express the following in exponential form:

   (i) $5 \times 5 \times 5 \times 5 \times 5$
   (ii) $4 \times 4 \times 4 \times 5 \times 5 \times 5$
   (iii) $(-1) \times (-1) \times (-1) \times (-1) \times (-1)$
   (iv) $a \times a \times a \times b \times c \times c \times c \times d \times d$

6. Express each of the following as product of powers of their prime factors:

   (i) 405
   (ii) 504
   (iii) 500

7. Simplify the following and write in exponential form:

   (i) $(5^2)^3$
   (ii) $(2^3)^3$
   (iii) $(a^b)^c$
   (iv) $[(5)^2]^2$

8. Express each of the following as a product of prime factors is the exponential form:

   (i) 729×125
   (ii) 384×147

9. Simplify the following:

   (i) $10^3 \times 9^0 + 3^3 \times 2 + 7^0$
   (ii) $6^3 \times 7^0 + (-3)^4 - 9^0$

10. Write the following in expanded form:

(i) 70,824
(ii) 1,69,835

11. Find the number from each of the expanded form:

(i) $7 \times 10^8 + 3 \times 10^5 + 7 \times 10^2 + 6 \times 10^1 + 9$
(ii) $4 \times 10^7 + 6 \times 10^3 + 5$

12. Find the value of

(a) $3^0 \div 4^0$
(b) $(8^0 - 2^0) \div (8^0 + 2^0)$
(c) $(2^0 + 3^0 + 4^0) - (4^0 - 3^0 - 2^0)$

13. Express the following in standard form:

(i) 8,19,00,000
(ii) 5,94,00,00,00,000
(iii) 6892.25

14. By what number should we multiply (2^{-5}) so that the product may be equal to (2^{-1})?

15. By what number should $(15)^{-3}$ be multiplied so that the product may be equal to $(15)^{-3}$?

16. By what number should $(24)^{-1}$ be divided so that the quotient may be equal to $(4)^{-1}$?

****

CHAPTER- 15:REPRESENTING 3D IN 2D

WORKSHEET - 15

1. **The vertical cut of a brick will show the cross section is**

   (a) circle

   (b) pentagon

   (c) rectangle

2. **The number of faces of a triangular prism is _______.**

   (a) 5

   (b) 6

   (c) 4

3. **The number of faces of a cube is _______.**

   (a) 4

   (b) 6

   (c) 8

4. **A cuboid has ________ rectangular faces.**

   (a) 8

   (b) 2

   (c) 6

5. **The number of faces of a cylinder is _______.**

   (a) 2

   (b) 1

   (c) None of these

6. **The number of faces of a square pyramid is _______.**

   (a) 4

   (b) 7

   (c) 5

7. **Identify the correct statement from the following.**

   (a) A triangle has 3 sides and 4 vertices.

(b) A cylinder has 3 faces.

(c) All sides of the rectangle are equal.

8. The number of faces of a rectangular prism is _______.

(a) 4

(b) 6

(c) 3

9. The number of edges of a square pyramid is _______.

(a) 4

(b) 6

(c) 8

10. The number of edges of a rectangular pyramid is _______.

(a) 21

(b) 8

(c) 7

11. The number of edges of a triangular pyramid is _______.

(a) 8

(b) 5

(c) 6

12. The number of faces of a triangular pyramid or tetrahedron is _______.

(a) 4

(b) 6

(c) 5

13. The number of triangular faces of a triangular prism is _______.

(a) 2
(b) 1
(c) 4

14. Cuboid is an example of

(a) Both

(b) 2-D shape

(c) 3-D shape

15. The number of vertices of a cube is _______.

(a) 12

(b) 8

(c) 6

16. Which of the following is the number of vertices of sphere?

(a) 0

(b) 1

(c) 2

17. A die is cut horizontally. What is the cross-section obtained?

(a) A triangle

(b) A rectangle

(c) A square

****

CHAPTER- 16:CONSTRUCTIONS

WORKSHEET - 16

1. Draw ΔPQR in which QR = 5.4 cm, $\angle Q = 40°$ and PR = 6.2 cm.
2. Draw an isosceles right-angled triangle whose hypotenuse is 5.8 cm.
3. Construct a ΔABC such that AB = 6.5 cm, AC = 5 cm and the altitude AP to BC is 4 cm.
4. Construct an equilateral triangle whose altitude is 4.5 cm.
5. Draw angles of the measures given below and draw their bisectors:

   i. 105°
   ii. 55°
   iii. 90°
6. Draw a right-angled triangle. Draw the perpendicular bisectors of its sides. Where does the point of concurrence lie?
7. Draw line segments of the lengths given below and draw their perpendicular bisectors:

   i. 5.3 cm
   ii. 6.7 cm
   iii. 3.8 cm
8. Construct a triangle ABC in which BC = 6 cm, CA = 5 cm and AB = 4 cm.
9. Construct a triangle PQR in which PQ = 5.8 cm, QR = 6.5 cm, PR = 4.5 cm.
10. Construct a triangle LMN in which LM = LN = 5.5 cm, MN = 7 cm.
11. Construct a triangle STU in which $\angle T = 60°$, $\angle U = 70°$ and TU = 7.5 cm.
12. Construct a right triangle ABC in which $\angle C = 90°$ and $\angle B = 45°$, CB = 5 cm.
13. Construct a right triangle XYZ in which $\angle Y = 90°$, XY = 5 cm and YZ = 7 cm.
14. Construct an equilateral triangle in which AB = BC = CA = 6 cm. What is the measure of its each angle?

****

CHAPTER- 17:DATA HANDING : COLLECTING AND ORGANISING DATA

WORKSHEET - 17

1. **Fill in the Blanks**

   i. A graph that uses lines to connect data points is called a __________.

   ii. The value that appears most frequently in a data set is called the __________.

   iii. The average of a data set is called the __________.

   iv. The process of collecting and organizing data is known as __________.

   v. A circular graph divided into sectors is called a __________.

2. **Find the range of height of any of the ten students of a class.**

   The height in cm of 10 students in a class = 130, 132, 135, 142, 137, 139, 140, 143, 145 & 148

   (Hint: Range of Heights is equal to be = Highest value – The lowest value)

3. **Determine the Mean of the first five whole numbers.**

   (Hint: Mean is equal to = (Sum of first five whole numbers) divided by (Total Number of whole numbers)

4. **A cricketer scores the following below runs in his eight innings: 58, 46, 76, 40, 35, 45, 0 and 100. Determine the mean score.**

   (Hint: Mean score is equal to = (Total runs scored by the cricketer in all innings) divided by (Total Number of innings)

5. **The marks out of 100 obtained by the group of students in the science test in their class are 85, 76, 90, 56, 95, 85, 39, 48, 81 and 75.**

   Now Find the:

   (a) Highest and lowest marks obtained by the students.

   (b) Range of the marks obtained.

   (c) Mean marks obtained by the student's group.

6. **The enrolment in a school during their six consecutive years is as follows:**

   1555, 1670, 1750, 2013, 2540 and 2820. Find the mean enrolment of their school for this period.

7. **The heights of ten girls were measured in cm, and then the results are given as follows:**

   135, 150, 139, 146, 128, 151, 132,149, 143 and 141.

(a) What is the height found of the tallest girl?
(b) What is the height of the shortest girl?
(c) What is the range of the data?
(d) What is the mean height found of the girls?
(e) How many girls have heights that are more than the mean height?

8. **The scores in a mathematics test (out of 25) of the 15 students in a class are as follows:**

19, 25, 10, 5, 16, 25, 23, 20, 9, 20, 15, 20, 24, 12 and 20
Find the Mode and the Median of this data. Are they the same?

9. **The runs scored in the cricket match by the 11 players are as follows:**

6, 15, 80, 120, 50, 100, 10, 15, 8, 10 and 15
Find the Mean, Mode and the Median of this data. Are these three same?

10. **The weights (in kg.) of 15 students present in a class are:**

38, 42, 43, 35, 37, 45, 50, 32, 43, 40, 36, 38, 43, 38 and 47

(i) Determine the Mode and Median of the above data.

(ii) Is there more than one Mode possible?

11. **Find both the Mode and Median of the given data: 13, 14, 19, 16, 12, 12, 14, 13, 14**

12. **Tell whether the following statement is true or false:**

(a) The Mode is always present as one of the numbers in the given data.

(Hint: the Mode is always one of the numbers present in the data.)

(b) The Mean is one of the numbers present in the data.

(Hint: the Mean may or may not be the one of the numbers present in the data.

(c) The Median is always present as one of the numbers in the data.

(Hint: the median is always one of the numbers present in a data)

(d) The data 6, 13, 9, 4, 3, 8, 9, and 12 have a mean of 9.

(Hint: Mean is equal to = Sum of all given observations divided by the total no of observations.)

13. **There are six marbles present in a box ranging with numbers from 1 to 6 marked on each one of them.**

(a) What is the major probability of drawing a marble with the number 2?

(b) What is the major probability of drawing a marble with the number 5?

14. **A coin is flipped to decide which of the two teams starts the game. What is the probability that team A will start?**

15. **Let x, y, and z denote three observations. The final Mean of these observations is**

(i) $(x \times y \times z)/3$ (ii) $(x + y + z)/3$

(iii) $(x - y - z)/3$ (iv) $(x \times y + z)/3$

Explanation – The average or the Arithmetic Mean or the Mean of the given data is the Sum of all of these observations divided by the number of observations.

16. **The number of trees present in different parts of a city is 33, 48,33, 34, 33, 34, 33 and 24. The Mode of the following data is**

(a) 24 (b) 34 (c) 33 (d) 48

Explanation- Mode is the observation which occurs most frequently in the data.

17. **Which measures of the central tendency get affected in the extreme observations of both of these ends of a data arranged in the descending order are removed?**

(i) Mean and mode (ii) Mean and Median

(iii) Mode and Median (iv) Mean, Median and Mode

****

CHAPTER-18: SYMMETRY

WORKSHEET - 18

1. Draw any two English alphabets having an only a vertical line of symmetry.

2. Draw any two English alphabets having a horizontal line of symmetry.

3. Draw any two English alphabets having both horizontal and vertical line of symmetry.

4. Dray any two English alphabets which has no line of symmetry.

5. Draw any two figures which have the order of rotational symmetry 4.

6. Draw any two figures which have the order of rotational symmetry 2.

7. Draw a figure having an infinite number of lines of symmetry. (Hint: circle)

8. How many lines of symmetry do the following have:

   (a) a parallelogram
   (b) an equilateral triangle
   (c) a right angle with equal legs
   (d) an angle with equal arms
   (e) a semicircle
   (f) a rhombus
   (g) a square
   (h) scalene triangle

9. What letters of the English alphabet have reflectional symmetry about

   (a) a vertical mirror
   (b) a horizontal mirror
   (c) both horizontal and vertical mirrors

10. A In A XYZ, XY = XZ and XM⊥YZand ZP⊥XY. About which of the following is the triangle symmetrical?

    (a) XM

    (b) YN

    (c) ZP

    (d) XZ

11. How many lines of symmetries are there in rectangle?

    (a) 2

    (b) 1

(c) 0

(d) None of these

12. How many lines of symmetries are there in an equilateral triangle?

(a) 2

(b) 3

(c) 0

(d) 1

13. Letter 'C' of the English alphabet have reflectional symmetry (i.e., symmetry related to mirror reflection) about.

(a) a horizontal mirror

(b) a vertical mirror

(c) both

(d) None of these

14. Letter 'H' of the English alphabet have reflectional symmetry (i.e., symmetry related to mirror reflection) about.

(a) A vertical mirror

(b) Both horizontal and vertical

(c) A horizontal mirror

(d) Neither horizontal nor vertical

15. Which of the following triangles has no line of symmetry?

(a) An equilateral triangle

(b) An isosceles triangle

(c) A scalene triangle

(d) All of the above

****

CHAPTER- 19: VISUALISING SOLID SHAPES

WORKSHEET - 19

1. If three cubes of dimensions 2 cm × 2 cm × 2 cm are placed end to end, what would be the dimension of the resulting cuboid?

2. **Answer the following:**

(i) Why a cone is not a pyramid?
(ii) How many dimension a solid have?
(iii) Name the solid having one curved and two flat faces but no vertex.
Solution:
(i) Cone is not a pyramid because its base is not a polygon.
(ii) Three.
(iii) Cylinder

3. Write down the number of edges on each of the following solid figures:

(i) Cube
(ii) Tetrahedron
(iii) Sphere
(iv) Triangular prism

4. What cross-section do you get when you give a horizontal cut to an ice cream cone?

5. **Name the solids that have:**

(i) 1 curved surface
(ii) 4 faces
(iii) 6 faces
(iv) 5 faces and 5 vertices
(v) 8 triangular faces
(vi) 6 triangular faces and 2 hexagonal faces.

****

SAMPLE PAPERS

Sample Paper - 1

MAX. MARKS: 80 **DURATION: 2½ HRS**

General Instructions:

(i) All questions are compulsory.

(ii) This question paper contains 23 questions divided into four Sections A, B, C and D.

(iii) Section A comprises 3 Questions (Fill in the Blanks, Multiple choice questions and do as direct) of 20 marks.

(iv) Section B comprises 8 questions of 2 marks each.

(v) Section C comprises 8 questions of 3 marks each.

(vi) Section D comprises 4 questions of 5 marks each.

SECTION – A

Question 1:

FILL IN THE BLANKS: (1 x 10 = 10)

1. $(-18) \times (-10) \times 9 =$ ________.
2. $\frac{1}{2}$ of 24 = _______.
3. Mean of first five whole number = ______.
4. Simple equation for the number b divided by 5 gives 6 = _______.
5. Each pair of interior angles on the same side of transversal are _________.
6. 6 bowls cost Rs 90. What would be the cost of 10 such bowls = _________.
7. The place value of 7 in 2.876 is =_________.
8. $\frac{3}{5}$ in percentage form = ________.
9. Two angles on a plane are called______ if they have common arm and common vertex.
10. The sum of the length of the sides of a triangle is known as _______.

Question 2:

Choose the correct answer: (1 x 5 = 5)

1. By joining any two points on the circumference of a circle we obtain
2. The sum of two angles of a right-angled triangle is
3. The smallest of the fractions $\frac{3}{5}, \frac{3}{8}, \frac{3}{4}, \frac{3}{2}$ is
4. An angle whose measure is 180^0 is called
5. $70 + 6 + \frac{3}{1000}$

Question 3:

Do as directed: (1 X 5 = 5)

1. Write the value of $\frac{239}{100}$ in decimals.
2. Write Hindu – Arabic numeral for XCI.
3. Write the predecessor of -69.
4. Write the prime factors of smallest 4- digit numbers.
5. Solve 764 X 331 + 764 X 169 using distributive property.

SECTION – B (2 Marks each)

Question 4:

If Manohar pays an interest of Rs 750 for 2 years on a sum of Rs 4,500, find the rate of interest.

Question 5:

Selling price of a toy car is Rs 540. If the profit made by shopkeeper is 20%, what is the cost price of this toy?

Question 6:

Solve and write the answer in exponential form:

$\left(\frac{3^7}{3^5}\right) \times 3^2$

Question 7: Express the number appearing in the following statements in standard form.

1. The distance between Earth and Moon is 384,000,000 m.
2. Speed of light in vacuum is 300,000,000 m/s.

Question 8: Find the value of p -4 = 5(p-2)

Question 9: How much less is 28.8 km than 42.3 km?

Question 10: The first three terms of a proportion are 3,5 and 21 respectively. Find its fourth term.

Question 11: Write the number of vertices, faces and edges of a cylinder.

Section – C (3 marks each)

Question 12: Write the expanded form for the following:

1. 279404
2. 20068

Question 13: Find the value of x and find the values of angles in the given figure given below.

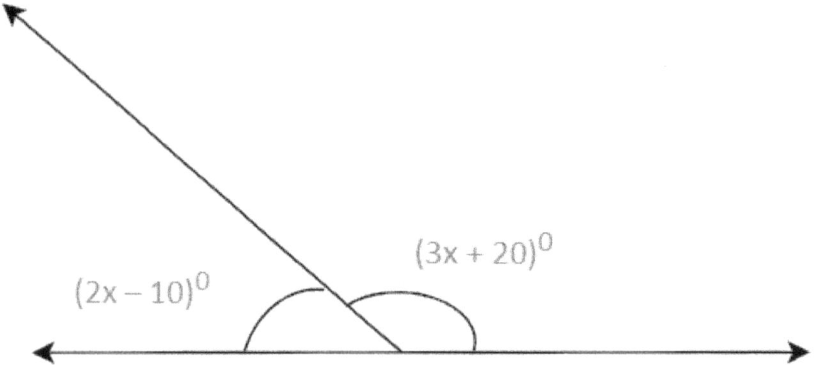

Question 14: Solve the following:

1. Irfan says that he has 7 marbles more than five times the marbles Parmit has. Irfan has 37 marbles. How many marbles does Parmit have?

2. Laxmi's father is 49 years old. He is 4 years older than three times Laxmi's age. What is Laxmi's age?

Question 15: The two sides of the parallelogram ABCD are 6 cm and 4 cm. The height corresponding to the base CD is 3 cm. Find the

1. Area of the parallelogram.
2. The height corresponding to the base AD.

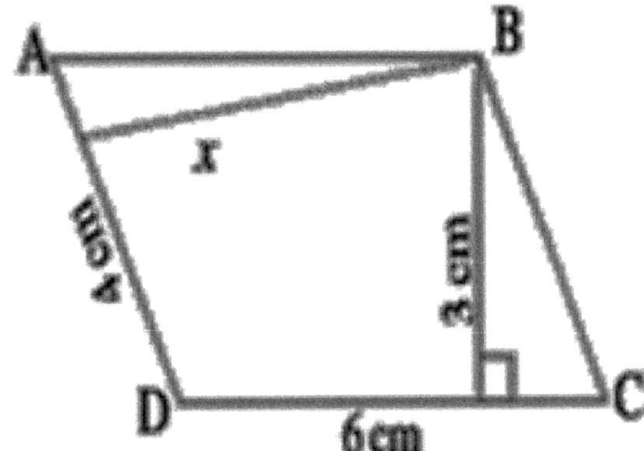

Question 16: List three rational numbers between – 2 and – 1.

Question 17: Reena's mother said, to make idlis, you must take two parts rice and one-part urad dal. What percentage of such a mixture would be rice and what percentage would be urad dal?

Question 18: Population of Rajasthan = 570 lakhs and population of U.P. = 1660 lakhs.

Area of Rajasthan = 3 lakh km^2 and area of U.P. = 2 lakh km^2.

(i) How many people are there per km2 in both states?

(ii) Which state is less populated?

Question 19: Find the mode and median of the data: 13, 16, 12, 14, 19, 12, 14, 13, 14.

Section – D (5 marks each)

Question 20: Vidya and Pratap went for a picnic. Their mother gave them a water bottle that contained 5 litres of water. Vidya consumed $\frac{2}{5}$ of the water. Pratap consumed the remaining water.

1. How much water did Vidya drink?
2. What fraction of the total quantity of water did Pratap drink?

Question 21: Find the value of x in each of the following figures if *l* // *m*.

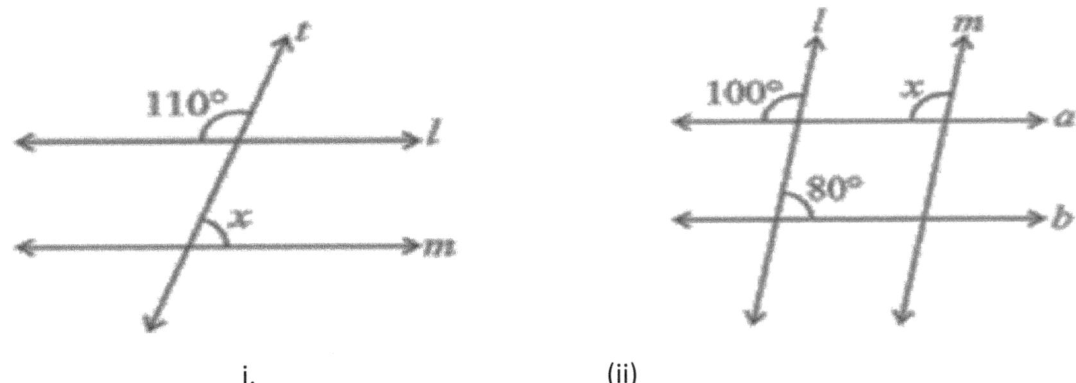

i. (ii)

Question 22: Tell what is the profit or loss in the following transactions. Also find profit per cent or loss per cent in each case.

1. Gardening shears bought for Rs 250 and sold for Rs 325.
2. A refrigerator bought for RS. 12,000 and sold at Rs. 13,500.

Question 23: Find the product, using suitable properties:

1. $26 \times (-48) + (-48) \times (-36)$
2. $8 \times 53 \times (-125)$
3. $15 \times (-25) \times (-4) \times (-10)$

****

Sample Paper - 2

MAX. MARKS: 80 **DURATION: 2½ HRS**

General Instructions:

(i). All questions are compulsory.
(ii). This question paper contains 23 questions divided into four Sections A, B, C and D.
(iii) Section A comprises 3 Questions (Fill in the Blanks, Multiple choice questions and Do as direct) of 20 marks.
(iv) Section B comprises 8 questions of 2 marks each.
(v) Section C comprises 8 questions of 3 marks each.
(vi) Section D comprises 4 questions of 5 marks each.

SECTION – A

Question 1:

FILL IN THE BLANKS: **(1 x 10 = 10)**

(a) (-25) X 8 + (-25) X 2 = ________.
(b) The supplement of angle 125^0 = ________.
(c) An exterior angle of a triangle is equal to the________ of its interior opposite angles.
(d) The sum of the interior angles of a triangle is = _______.
(e) 3n +7 = 25, n = _______.
(f) Line which cuts two parallel lines is called ______.
(g) Fractions which have denominators greater than numerators are called______ fractions.
(h) Ratio of 15 Kg to 210g = ______.
(i) Area of square whose perimeter is 320 cm = ________.
(j) Express 128 as a power of 2= ________.

Question 2:

Choose the correct answer: (1 x 5 = 5)

1. If $\frac{x}{6} = \frac{7}{-3}$, then the value of x is

(a) -14

(b) 14

(c) 21

(d) - 21

2. $\frac{3}{4}$ as rate percent is

(a) 7.5 %

(b) 75 %

(c) 0.75 %

(d) none of these

3. The area of a rectangular sheet is 300 cm^2, if the length of sheet is 25 cm, then width of the sheet is

(a) 36 cm

(b) 12 cm

(c) 50 cm

(d) 20 cm

4. A Cuboid has

(a) 8 vertices

(b) 12 vertices

(c) 6 vertices

(d) 7 vertices

5. The value of 3a – b + 4 – (a – b)

(a) 2a – 4

(b) 2a + 4

(c) -2a + 4

(d) -2a -4

Question 3: Do as Directed: (1 X 5 = 5)

1. A cricketer scores the following runs in eight innings: 58, 76, 40, 35, 46, 45, 0, 100. Find the mean score.
2. Find the value of $2 - \frac{3}{5}$.
3. Write 0.09 in the percentage form.
4. Express 1000 as a product of power of prime factors.
5. 12 p – 5 = 5, Find the value of p.

SECTION – B (2 Marks each)

Question 4: Is there a triangle whose sides have lengths 10.2 cm, 5.8 cm and 4.5 cm?

Question 5: Find $\frac{2}{3}$ of 18 and 27.

Question 6: Express $\frac{-3}{8}$ as a rational number with

1. Denominator = 32
2. Denominator = -40

Question 7: Simplify $(-2)^3 \times (-10)^3$

Question 8: If I take three-fourths of a number and add 3 to it, I get 21. Find the number.

Question 9: Give four rational numbers equivalent to $\frac{5}{-3}$.

Question 10: State the number of lines of symmetry for the following figures.

1. An Equilateral triangle
2. A square
3. A Circle
4. A regular hexagon

Question 11: Find the angle which is equal to its complement.

SECTION – C (3 Marks each)

Question 12: Solve the following:

1. $7m + \frac{19}{2} = 13$
2. $\frac{q}{4} + 7 = 5$

Question 13:

Express the following numbers in the standard form:

1. 5985.3
2. 65,950
3. 70,040,000,000

Question 14:

1. The sum of two integers is – 55. If one of them is 80, Find the other?

2. Write all integers from 0 to -6 in increasing order.

Question 15:

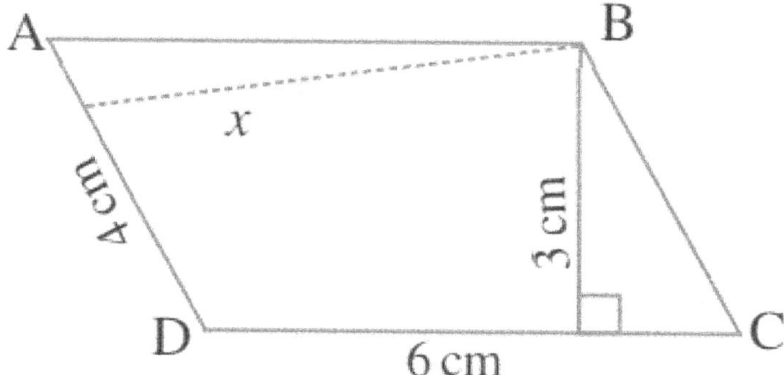

The two sides of the parallelogram ABCD are 6 cm and 4 cm. The height corresponding to the base CD is 3 cm. Find the

(a) area of the parallelogram.

(b) the height corresponding to the base AD.

Question 16:

Simplify:

(a) $(2)^3 \times (a)^3 \times 5a^4$

(b) $\dfrac{(12)^4 \times (9)^3 \times 4}{(6)^3 \times 8^2 \times 27}$

Question 17:

Rs7,000 is borrowed at 3.5% rate of interest p.a. borrowed for 2 years. Find the amount to be paid at the end of the second year.

Question 18:

Multiply and reduce to lowest form and convert into a mixed fraction:

1. $20 \times \frac{4}{5}$
2. $13 \times \frac{1}{3}$
3. $15 \times \frac{3}{5}$

Question 19:

The heights of 10 girls were measured in cm and the results are as follows: 135, 150, 139, 128, 151, 132, 146, 149, 143, 141.

1. What is the height of the tallest girl?
2. What is the height of the shortest girl?
3. What is the range of the data?
4. How many girls have heights more than the mean height?

SECTION – D (5 marks each)

Question 20:

In a class test containing 15 questions, 4 marks are given for every correct answer and (-(-2) marks are given for every incorrect answer.

1. Gurpreet attempts all questions but only 9 of her answers are correct. What is her total score?
2. One of her friends gets only 5 answers correct. What will be her score?

Question 21:

(a) From the sum of 3x – y + 11 and – y – 11, subtract 3x – y - 11

(b) From the sum of 4 + 3x and 5 – x + 2x2, subtract the sum of 3x2 – 5y and –x2 + 2x + 5

Question 22:

If 250 is to be divided amongst Ravi, Raju and Roy, so that Ravi gets two parts, Raju three parts and Roy five parts.

How much money will each get? What will it be in percentages?

Question 23:

Tell whether the following is certain to happen, impossible, can happen but not certain.

1. You are older today than yesterday.
2. A tossed coin will land heads up.
3. A die when tossed shall land up with 8 on top.
4. The next traffic light seen will be green.
5. Tomorrow will be a cloudy day.

****

Sample paper - 3

MAX. MARKS: 80 **DURATION: 2½ HRS**

General Instructions:

(i). All questions are compulsory.
(ii). This question paper contains 23 questions divided into four Sections A, B, C and D.
(iii) Section A comprises 3 Questions (Fill in the Blanks, Multiple choice questions and Do as direct) of 20 marks.
(iv) Section B comprises 8 questions of 2 marks each.
(v) Section C comprises 8 questions of 3 marks each.
(vi) Section D comprises 4 questions of 5 marks each.

Section – A (1 mark each)

Multiple Choice Questions:

Question 1:

(-25) X 8 + (-25) x 2 =?

(a) 250 (b) 150 (c) – 250 (d) -150

Question 2:

The fraction equivalent to $\frac{2}{13}$ is

(a) $\frac{10}{3}$ (b) $\frac{3}{5}$ (c) $\frac{10}{6}$ (d) $\frac{6}{10}$

Question 3:

When 0.48 is written in the simplest form of its terms, the sum of its numerator and denominator is

(a) 148 (b) 74 (c) 37 (d) 147

Question 4:

$-\frac{102}{119}$ in standard form is

(a) $-\frac{6}{7}$ (b) $\frac{6}{7}$ (c) $-\frac{6}{17}$ (d) none of these

Question 5:

$1 \div \div \frac{1}{3} =$

(a) $\frac{1}{3}$ (b) 3 (c) $1\frac{1}{3}$ (d) $3\frac{1}{3}$

Question 6:

The number 4,70,394 in standard form is written as

(a) 4.70394×10^5 (b) 4.70394×10^4 (c) 47.0394×10^4 (d) 4703.94×10^2

Question 7:

The sum of the coefficients in the terms of $2x^2y - 3xy^2 + 4xy$ is

(a) -3 (b) 3 (c) 9 (d) 5

Question 8:

The zero of 3x + 2 is

(a) $\frac{2}{3}$ (b) $\frac{3}{2}$ (c) $-\frac{2}{3}$ (d) $-\frac{3}{2}$

Question 9:

The boys and girls in a school are in the ratio 9: 5. If the number girls is 320, then the total strength of the school is

(a) 840 (b) 896 (c) 920 (d) 576

Question 10:

If the cost of 15 mangoes is ₹ 180, then what is the cost of 25 mangoes?

(a) 220 (b) 360 (c) 200 (d) 300

Section – B (2 marks each)

Question 11:

Find 30% of ₹ 180

Question 12:

Harmeet purchased 4.5kg of potatoes at the rate of Rs.23.75 per kg. How much money should she pay in nearest rupees?

Question 13:

Find a number, such that when I subtracted 11 from twice a number, the result was 15.

Question 14:

Find the area, in hectare, of a field whose length is 240 m and breadth 110 m.

Question 15:

If the cost price of 6 pencils is equal to the selling price of 5 pencils. Find the gain percent.

Question 16:

Divide ₹ 840 between Amit and Tanvy in the ratio 5: 7.

Question 17:

In what time will ₹ 3600 amount to ₹ 4320 at 8% per annum simple interest?

Question 18:

Express $\frac{-5}{13}$ as a rational number with positive numerator.

Question 19:

If the cost of $5\frac{2}{5}$ litres of milk is ₹ $101\frac{1}{4}$. Find its cost per litre.

Question 20:

A certain freezing process requires that room temperature be lowered from 40^0C at the rate of 5^0C per hour. What will be the room temperature 12 hours after the process begins?

Section – C (4 marks each)

Question 21:

Find the values of the angles x, y, and z in the given figure:

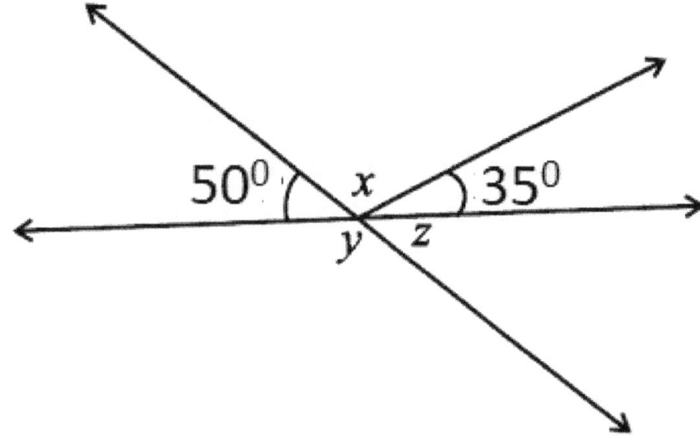

Question 22:

In the below figure, if y is five times x, find the value of z.

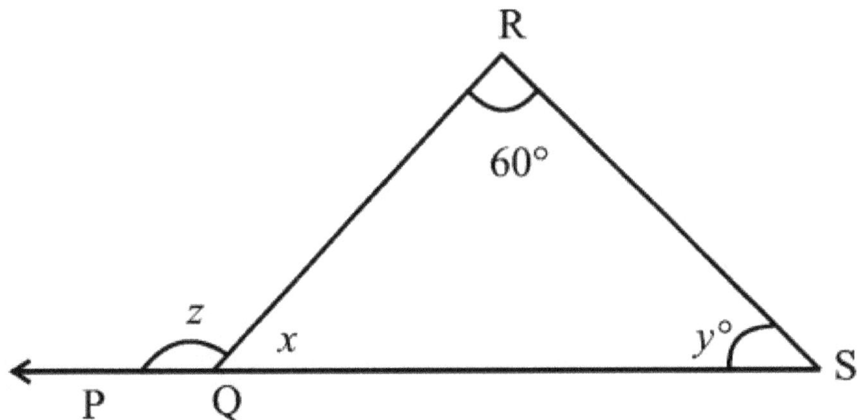

Question 23:

The product of two rational numbers is $\frac{-8}{9}$. If one of the numbers is $-\frac{-4}{15}$. Find the other.

Question 24:

The sum of three consecutive integers is 5 more than the smallest of the integers. Find the integers.

Question 25:

The area of a right triangle is 40 cm^2. If one of its legs measures 8 cm. Find the length of the other leg.

Section – D (5 marks each)

Question 26:

The runs scored in a cricket match by 11 players is as follows:

6, 15, 120, 50, 100, 80, 10, 15, 8, 10, 15

Find the mean, mode and median of this data.

Question 27:

A tree is broken at a height of 5 m from the ground and its top touches the ground at a distance of 12 m from the base of the tree. Find the original height of the tree.

Question 28:

How much is $x^3 - 2x^2 + x + 4$ greater than $2x^3 + 7x^2 - 5x + 6$?

Question 29:

A sum of money at simple interest doubles itself in 8 years 4 months. In how much time will it treble itself.

Question 30:

The performance of students in 1st Term and 2nd Term is given. Draw a double bar graph choosing appropriate scale and answer the following:

(i) In which subject, has the child improved his performance the most?

(ii) In which subject is the improvement the least?

(iii) Has the performance gone down in any subject?

Subject	English	Hindi	Maths	Science	S.Science
1st Term (M.M. 100)	62	72	88	81	73
2nd Term (M.M. 100)	70	65	95	85	75

Question 31:

A bag contains ₹ 187 in the form of 1 rupee, 50 paise and 10 paise coins in the ratio 3:4:5. Find the number of each type of coins.

****

Sample Paper - 4

MAX. MARKS: 80 **DURATION: 2½ HRS**

General Instructions:

(i) All questions are compulsory.

(ii) This question paper contains 23 questions divided into four Sections A, B, C and D.

(iii) Section A comprises 3 Questions (Fill in the Blanks, Multiple choice questions and do as direct) of 20 marks.

(iv) Section B comprises 8 questions of 2 marks each.

(v) Section C comprises 8 questions of 3 marks each.

(vi) Section D comprises 4 questions of 5 marks each.

SECTION – A

Question 1:FILL IN THE BLANKS: (1 x 10 = 10)

1. $(-18) \times (-10) \times 9 =$ ________.
2. $\frac{1}{2}$ of 24 = ________.
3. Mean of first five whole number = _______.
4. Simple equation for the number b divided by 5 gives 6 = _______.
5. Each pair of interior angles on the same side of transversal are _________.
6. 6 bowls cost Rs 90. What would be the cost of 10 such bowls = _________.
7. The place value of 7 in 2.876 is =_________.
8. $\frac{3}{5}$ in percentage form = ________.
9. Two angles on a plane are called______ if they have common arm and common vertex.
10. The sum of the length of the sides of a triangle is known as _______.

Question 2:

Choose the correct answer: (1 x 5 = 5)

1. By joining any two points on the circumference of a circle we obtain

2. The sum of two angles of a right-angled triangle is

3. The smallest of the fractions $\frac{3}{5}, \frac{3}{8}, \frac{3}{4}, \frac{3}{2}$ is

4. An angle whose measure is 180^0 is called

5. $70 + 6 + \frac{3}{1000}$

Question 3:

Do as directed: (1 X 5 = 5)

1. Write the value of $\frac{239}{100}$ in decimals.
2. Write Hindu – Arabic numeral for XCI.
3. Write the predecessor of -69.
4. Write the prime factors of smallest 4- digit numbers.
5. Solve 764 X 331 + 764 X 169 using distributive property.

SECTION – B (2 Marks each)

Question 4:

If Manohar pays an interest of Rs 750 for 2 years on a sum of Rs 4,500, find the rate of interest.

Question 5:

Selling price of a toy car is Rs 540. If the profit made by shopkeeper is 20%, what is the cost price of this toy?

Question 6:

Solve and write the answer in exponential form:

$\left(\frac{3^7}{3^5}\right) \times 3^2$

Question 7:

Express the number appearing in the following statements in standard form.

1. The distance between Earth and Moon is 384,000,000 m.
2. Speed of light in vacuum is 300,000,000 m/s.

Question 8:

Find the value of p.

-4 = 5(p-2)

Question 9:

How much less is 28.8 km than 42.3 km?

Question 10.

The first three terms of a proportion are 3,5 and 21 respectively. Find its fourth term.

Question 11.

Write the number of vertices, faces and edges of a cylinder.

Section – C (3 marks each)

Question 12.

Write the expanded form for the following:

1. 279404
2. 20068

Question 13.

Find the value of x and find the values of angles in the given figure given below.

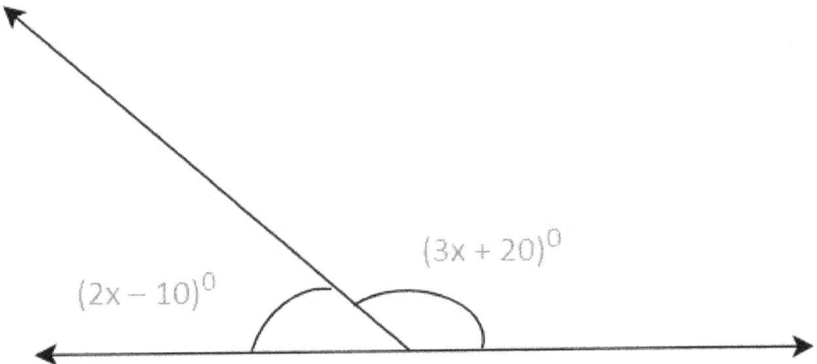

Question 14:

Solve the following:

1. Irfan says that he has 7 marbles more than five times the marbles Parmit has. Irfan has 37 marbles. How many marbles does Parmit have?
2. Laxmi's father is 49 years old. He is 4 years older than three times Laxmi's age. What is Laxmi's age?

Question 15:

The two sides of the parallelogram ABCD are 6 cm and 4 cm. The height corresponding to the base CD is 3 cm. Find the

1. Area of the parallelogram.
2. The height corresponding to the base AD.

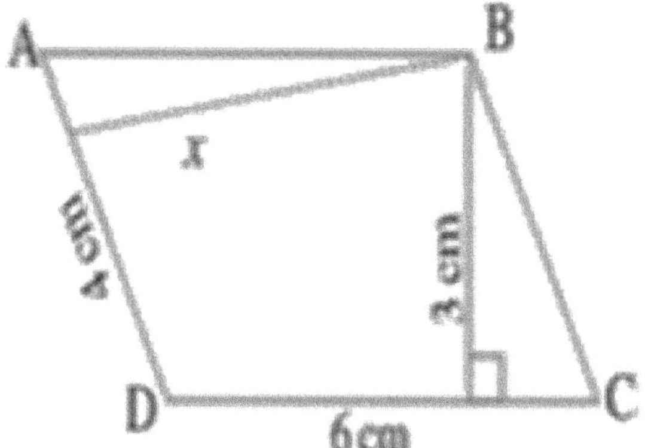

Question 16:

List three rational numbers between – 2 and – 1.

Question 17:

Reena's mother said, to make idlis, you must take two parts rice and one-part urad dal. What percentage of such a mixture would be rice and what percentage would be urad dal?

Question 18:

Population of Rajasthan = 570 lakhs and population of U.P. = 1660 lakhs.
Area of Rajasthan = 3 lakh km^2 and area of U.P. = 2 lakh km^2.
(i) How many people are there per km2 in both states?
(ii) Which state is less populated?

Question 19:

Find the mode and median of the data: 13, 16, 12, 14, 19, 12, 14, 13, 14.

Section – D (5 marks each)

Question 20:

Vidya and Pratap went for a picnic. Their mother gave them a water bottle that contained 5 litres of water. Vidya consumed $\frac{2}{5}$ of the water. Pratap consumed the remaining water.

1. How much water did Vidya drink?

2. What fraction of the total quantity of water did Pratap drink?

Question 21:

Find the value of x in each of the following figures if *l* // *m*.

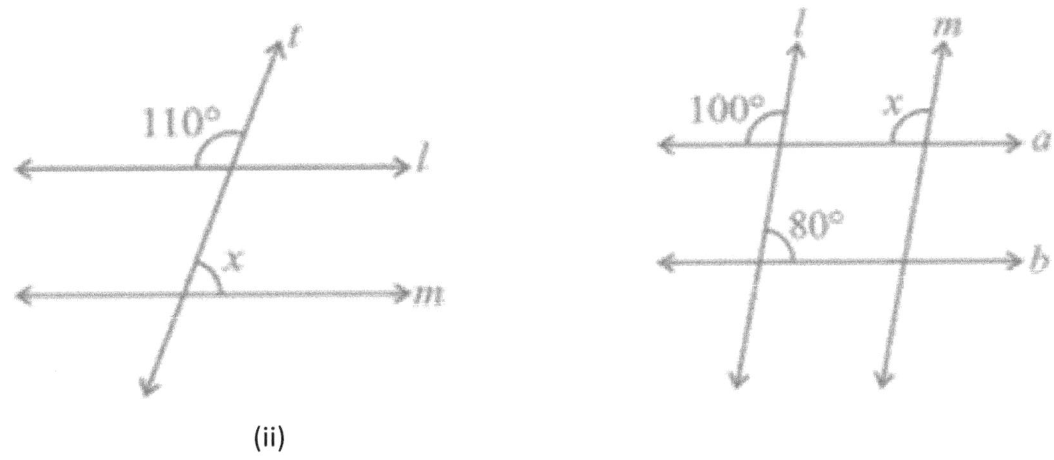

i. (ii)

Question 22:

Tell what is the profit or loss in the following transactions. Also find profit per cent or loss per cent in each case.

1. Gardening shears bought for Rs 250 and sold for Rs 325.

2. A refrigerator bought for RS. 12,000 and sold at Rs. 13,500.

Question 23:

Find the product, using suitable properties:

1. 26 × (– 48) + (– 48) × (–36)

2. 8 × 53 × (–125)

3. 15 × (–25) × (– 4) × (–10)

****

Reference:

- Ncert book
- R D Sharma
- https://www.champstreet.com/ncert-solutions/class-7/math/chapter-6/triangles-and-properties.jsp
- https://ncert.nic.in/textbook.php?lemh2=0-7
- https://opjsrgh.in/Content/Worksheet/PRACTICE-WS/2022-2023/day14/7-MATHEMATICS.pdf
- https://www.letsplaymaths.com/Class-7-Linear-Equations.html
- https://www.letsplaymaths.com/Class-7-Linear-Equations.html#C7
- https://www.geeksforgeeks.org/congruence-of-triangles/
- https://www.learncbse.in/congruence-of-triangles-class-7-extra-questions/

"Believe in yourself and rock in your exams!"

www.ingramcontent.com/pod-product-compliance
Lightning Source LLC
LaVergne TN
LVHW070942160826
845679LV00022B/1882

* 9 7 9 8 8 9 6 7 3 8 6 7 1 *